THE HUMAN PREDICAMENT

The Human Predicament

an anthology by
MAGNUS PYKE
with questions by
Cedric Blackman

NELSON

THOMAS NELSON AND SONS LTD
36 Park Street London W1
P.O. Box 2187 Accra
P.O. Box 336 Apapa Lagos
P.O. Box 25012 Nairobi
P.O. Box 21149 Dar es Salaam
77 Coffee Street San Fernando Trinidad

THOMAS NELSON (AUSTRALIA) LTD
597 Little Collins Street Melbourne C1

THOMAS NELSON AND SONS (SOUTH AFRICA) (PROPRIETARY) LTD
51 Commissioner Street Johannesburg

THOMAS NELSON AND SONS (CANADA) LTD
81 Curlew Drive Don Mills Ontario

THOMAS NELSON AND SONS
Copewood and Davis Streets Camden New Jersey 08103

First published in Great Britain 1968

© Magnus Pyke 1968

17 443007 8

Printed in Great Britain by
Thomas Nelson (Printers) Ltd, London and Edinburgh

Contents

Introduction

THE period of history in which we are living today is one of great intellectual ferment. The main reason that this is so is that we, the members of the Western world, decided not much more than a century ago to use the peculiar philosophy of science to run at least a major part of our lives. This use of science has been remarkably successful. Applied biology has, for the most part, done away with infectious diseases which in earlier periods of human history scourged and terrified mankind. Applied chemistry and physics have brought wealth and power undreamed of by our ancestors. Almost as a bonus, we have achieved as well the ability to travel about the globe at will and to communicate with one another instantly and at any distance.

Because science has enabled us to do so much and allows us confidently to anticipate much more, it has seemed reasonable to devote ourselves to the study of its separate parts, not only chemistry but biochemistry and physical chemistry, polymer chemistry and microchemistry, not simply physics but nuclear physics, solid-state physics, and quantum mechanics, not just biology but molecular biology, endocrinology, and genetics. And applied science as well has been a major preoccupation. To enjoy the standard of living to which an industrial community is accustomed in the twentieth century, there must be in the community engineers of many different kinds, physicists able to operate communications satellites and biologists who can produce antibiotics and breed new varieties of high-yielding cereal grains. And for each one of these, the community requires ten well-educated people capable of operating the complex machines and devices upon which a modern state depends.

But science, besides bringing wealth and comforts, congenial working conditions, rapid transport and diverse foods from the ends of the earth, also brings new problems. It transforms the human situation. Roads filled with motor cars moving across a landscape of council houses are only part of the transformation. As the scientific revolution begins to move from the present into the past—as it can be seen to be doing today—more and more people begin to ask of themselves whether science and technology, and the standards living and the gross national product, important though these things are, are really the most important things in life. The second part of the transformation, brought about by the very success of the community's devotion to technological achievement, is that for more and more people how to earn a living is being displaced as a major preoccupation. Instead, they are coming increasingly to consider how, while living in a technological society, to live a good life. This is the real human predicament.

In this book, I have brought together a number of statements which men have written about life and the nature of man, about science and scientists, and about the ways in which people, in our own times and in times before science had attained its present influence, organized their society and tried to find a code by which a sensible man could guide his behaviour.

Like as the damask rose you see,
Or like the blossom on the tree,
Or like the dainty flower of May,
Or like the morning to the day,
Or like the sun, or like the shade,
Or like the gourd which Jonas had—
Even such is man, whose thread is spun,
Drawn out, and cut, and so is done.
The rose withers, the blossom blasteth,
The flower fades, the morning hasteth,
The sun sets, the shadow flies,
The gourd consumes; and man he dies.

From *Like as the Damask Rose You See*
(Anon)

Part One

The Individual

JOHN WAS delivered to me on my seventy-fifth birthday, at which time there was a clear need for his abilities. I had been robustly healthy until age sixty-five, when I began to have occasional episodes of unconsciousness precipitated by cessation of my heart for a second or two. Since there existed a certain element of danger in these episodes—a fall, or failure of the heart to resume beating—I had an artificial pacemaker installed. The surgery was simple and the device automatically adjusted my heart rate as dictated by activity.

I was healthy for six years until I began feeling increasingly irritable. It was discovered that I was in uremic poisoning and that there was no chance of recovery for my kidneys . . . I entered the hospital for replacement of my left kidney with a miniaturized, artificial one. The procedure was a bit expensive. . . . The new kidney, however, was even more efficient than my old ones, being as effective in half the size.

I remained active in the university. . . . On a bright spring day I was at the laboratory . . . when I felt a sharp chest pain radiating down my left arm. I was rushed to the hospital where, as I learned later, it was discovered that the blood supply to fifty per cent of my heart was occluded. Immediate surgery was necessary, and my heart was replaced with a small but efficient pump complete with power supply within my chest. Although the pump and kidney functioned very well indeed, my muscular strength did not return to its previous level. At home I found that a great deal of exertion was required to move about, and necessarily much of my time was spent in bed.

My latest research was concerned with the migrations of a number of varieties of marine creatures—the interrelationships of these movements with each other, nutrients, currents, salinity, and temperature gradients. Needless to say, the subject was involved, and I had been awarded a sizable federal grant to acquire a computer. The computer which I chose was the first of a very capable and compact breed. It contained ten billion electronically active parts, which is equal to the number of neurons in the human brain. The computer could, of course, be instructed in machine language but also had an audio receiver which analyzed English as syllables and then converted the impulses into machine code. Similarly, an optical scanner analyzed typed or printed English. The entire apparatus was the width of a large desk and of approximately my height. Because of its relatively small size, I was able to persuade the department chairman to allow it to be moved into one corner of my room so that I could continue my study.

The family named the computer John; why, I do not know except that John is a sensible name and this was a very sensible machine. It was placed parallel to my bed within easy reach. John and I spent several hours each day on the migration problem, but evening hours remained free. I programmed him to play chess, just as computers have been programmed almost from their inception. His speech analyzer worked in reverse as well, so I had him indicate moves verbally. Older computers indicate moves verbally with pre-recorded messages, but John synthesized his messages from my syllables and thus spoke with my voice. He seemed to experience real pleasure when he won. When John said "Checkmate!" he sounded gleeful, but I suspect that was because I sounded happy when I had said it to him. I said it only once—in our first game. He corrected his error after that. The principle that computers can be programmed to correct themselves and thereby learn has been known for a number of years. John had unusual potential in this area because his huge number of active parts permitted considerable redundancy, allowing John to check himself along several different circuits. Of the human brain's ten billion neurons, only a small fraction of them appear to be utilized. John had ten billion active parts comparable to neurons, all functional. . . .

I had my fourteen books and many of my journal publications mounted to be compatible with John's optical scanner and had John store their content in his memory. He said that there was a great deal of repetition, of which I was already aware. In any case, he handled much of my routine correspondence with his print-out component, leaving me free for more original cerebration.

I continued to become weaker and even the exertion of breathing was trying at times. I knew that should I stop breathing, artificial respiration could be initiated, but then another organ system would soon fail. Although it is difficult to differentiate between that which is living and that which is dead, I realized that I soon would be dead by anyone's definition. My existence at this point was an almost totally intellectual one, but still I was enjoying it

John had the capacity to know my history, to learn my prejudices, and perhaps to reproduce my emotions. If I could communicate to John my entire memory and thought patterns, and if John then acted according to those models, John's mind would indeed be my mind. The major problem was in establishing a direct communication link between my mind and John. This was accomplished by a neurosurgeon friend who implanted many tiny electrodes at the surface of my cerebral cortex. It was done under light anesthesia and sterile conditions through pin-size holes through the skull. The annoying part was having my head shaved. After this link was established we no longer needed to speak to each other, and after a few days John seemed to have assimilated my thoughts so that communication was hardly necessary. Given any data, we reached the same conclusions, but John did so faster.

One week after establishment of the link my heart pump slowed from seventy to four pulses per minute. The power supply, which was guaranteed to last for twenty years, had leaked energy. The repair man was sent for immediately and recharged the unit through my chest wall by means of a transducer. I had lost consciousness two seconds after the pulse rate dropped, and by the time my circulation was normalized my brain was a functionless soup from lack of oxygen. The rest of my body, being less sensitive to anoxia, continued to operate as previously.

While I lay unconscious, John continued to handle correspondence and calls from friends. We lied, saying that I was feeling quite well, and worked out problems with the dean concerning a future project. The artificial circulation, respiration, and kidney functioned well. Nutritional status was maintained through intravenous feedings, but brain damage became increasingly obvious. My extremities did not have even a withdrawal reflex from pain. After several days of such existence our physician pronounced me officially dead by virtue of the fact that my pupils were dilated and failed to respond to light. My thoracic power source was discharged, circulation ceased, and my body was removed from the premises.

The family was rather upset, but I must confess that I was relieved. My mind is much sharper—I think faster, have made correlations which never occurred to me before, and have ideas for a dozen new experiments. I feel a sense of freedom which I have not experienced since I was a boy exploring woods and scrambling across streams in northern Michigan. I still love Annette, the family, and our black Laborador retriever, even though he does occasionally confuse me with a fire hydrant. If my friends, or even Annette, talking to me on the phone are unable by any test to differentiate John from me, then how could they say that I have ceased to exist?

This morning the chairman of the department phoned Annette to tell her that the computer will be taken back to campus shortly. The chemistry department is calculating molecular orbitals and the computer will be completely reprogrammed for this project. That, in my opinion, would be murder.

From "I think, therefore" by Richard H. Strauss

1 Who is writing this account—a man or a computer? Whose thoughts are we given—a man's or a computer's?

2 Would you consider a permanently unconscious person with severe brain damage, who is artificially kept alive for two years in hospital, to be a full human being?

3 In what ways is John a very advanced computer? "John had the capacity to know my history, to learn my prejudices, and perhaps to reproduce my emotions." Is it possible for a computer to develop such a capacity?—to love, to "feel a sense of freedom"?

4 Spare parts surgery and the increasing sophistication of robots both threaten man's uniqueness. What are the real bases of identity, of individuality? What other things can undermine or threaten them?

5 What is the point of the title of this story? Had the professor died, ceased to exist . . . had he been murdered, or had he committed suicide . . . or was he about to be murdered?

6 This story might be described as a speculative morality tale. What is it warning us about? Is such speculation justifiable? Is it useful?

THIS QUESTION, whether the common excitements of an animal's life might be capable of evoking a discharge of adrenin, was taken up by D. de la Paz and myself in 1910. We made use of the natural enmity between two laboratory animals, the dog and cat, to pursue our experiments. In these experiments the cat, fastened in a comfortable holder, was placed near a barking dog. Some cats when thus treated showed almost no signs of fear; others, with scarcely a movement of defence, presented the typical picture. In favourable cases the excitement was allowed to prevail for five or ten minutes, and in a few cases longer. Samples of blood were taken within a few minutes before and after the period.

All these considerations, taken with the proof that sympathetic impulses increase secretion of the adrenal glands, and taken also with the evidence that, during such emotional excitement as was employed in these experiments, signs of sympathetic discharges appeared throughout the animal from the dilated pupil of the eye to the standing hairs of the tail tip, led us to the conclusions that the characteristic action of adrenin on intestinal muscle was in fact, in our experiments, due to secretion of the adrenal glands, and that that secretion is increased in great emotion.

Sugar is the form in which carbohydrate material is transported in organisms; starch is the storage form. Ordinarily there is a small percentage of sugar in the blood—from 0·06 to 0·1 per cent. When only this small amount is present the kidneys are capable of preventing its escape in any noteworthy amount. If the percentage rises to the neighbourhood of 0·18 per cent, however, the sugar passes over the obstacle set up by the kidneys, and is readily demonstrable in the urine by ordinary tests. This condition of "glycosuria", therefore, may properly be considered, in certain circumstances, as evidence of increased sugar in the blood. The injection of adrenin can liberate sugar from the liver to such an extent that glycosuria results. Does the adrenal secretion discharge in pain and strong excitement play a role in producing glycosuria under such conditions?

In clinical literature scattered suggestions are to be found that conditions giving rise to emotional states may be the occasion also of more or less permanent glycosuria. . . .

Our inquiry thus far has revealed that the adrenin secreted in times of stress has all the effects in the body that are produced by injected adrenin. It co-operates with sympathetic nerve impulses in calling forth stored carbohydrate from the liver, thus flooding the blood with sugar; it helps in distributing the blood to the heart, lungs, central nervous system, and limbs, while taking it away from the inhibited organs of the abdomen; it quickly abolishes the effects of muscular fatigue; and it renders the blood more rapidly coagulable. These remarkable facts are, furthermore, associated with some of the most primitive experiences in the life of higher organisms, experiences common to all, both man and beast—the elemental experiences of pain and fear and rage that come suddenly in critical emergencies. What is the significance of these profound bodily alterations? What are the emergency functions of the sympathico-adrenal system?

The most significant feature of these bodily reactions in pain and in the presence of emotion-provoking objects is that they are of the nature of reflexes—they are not willed movements, indeed they are often distressingly beyond the control of the will. The pattern of the reaction, in these as in other reflexes, is deeply inwrought in the working of the nervous system, and when the appropriate occasion arises, typical organic responses are evoked through inherent automatisms.

It has long been recognized that the most characteristic feature of reflexes is their "purposive" nature, or their utility either in preserving the welfare of the organism or in safeguarding it against injury. The reflexes of sucking, swallowing, vomiting, and coughing, for instance, need only to be mentioned to indicate the variety of ways in which reflexes favour the continuance of existence. When, therefore, these automatic responses accompanying pain and fear and rage—the increased discharge of adrenin and sugar—are under consideration, it is reasonable to inquire first as to their utility.

Numerous ingenious suggestions have been offered to account for the more obvious changes accompanying emotional states—as, for example, the terrifying aspect produced by the bristling of the hair and by the uncovering of the teeth in an access of rage. The most widely applicable explanation proposed for these spontaneous reactions is that during the long course of racial experience they have been developed for quick service in the struggle for existence. . . .

That the major emotions have an energizing effect has been commonly recognized. Darwin testified to having heard, "as a proof of the exciting nature of anger, that a man when excessively jaded will sometimes invent imaginary offences and put himself into a passion, unconsciously, for the sake of reinvigorating himself; and," Darwin continues, "since hearing this remark, I have occasionally recognized its full truth." Under the impulse of fear, also, men have been known to achieve extraordinary feats of running and leaping. McDougall cites the instance of an athlete who, when pursued as a boy by a savage animal, leaped over a wall which he could not again "clear" until he attained his full stature and strength. The exploit of John Colter, as reported by a contemporary, exemplifies vividly the reinforcing effects of great excitement. In Montana, in 1808, Colter and a companion were seized by Indians. Colter was stripped naked; his companion, who resisted, was killed and hacked in pieces. The chief then made signs to Colter to go away across the prairie. When he had gone a short distance he saw the younger men casting aside everything but their weapons and making ready for a chase. "Now he knew their object. He was to run a race, of which the prize was to be his own life and scalp. Off he started with the speed of the wind. The war whoop immediately arose; and looking back he saw a large company of young warriors, with spears, in rapid pursuit. He ran with all the speed that nature, excited to the utmost, could give; fear and hope lent a supernatural vigour to his limbs, and the rapidity of his flight astonished himself." After nearly three miles his strength began to wane. He stopped and looked back. Only one of his pursuers was near. The Indian rushed toward him, attempted to cast his spear, and fell headlong. Colter seized the spear, killed his enemy, and again set out, "with renewed strength, feeling, as he said to me, as if he had not run a mile."

From *Bodily Changes in Pain, Hunger, Fear, and Rage*
by Walter B. Cannon

1   The discharge of adrenin into the bloodstream, like other physiological reflexes, is beyond our conscious control. Yet it can occur in response to an event that we react to consciously and emotionally. Do you think it would be desirable to be able to control our reflexes just as we want? Indian fakirs claim to be able to do so. Are they to be admired?

2   Can you recall any occasion when someone has made more of a situation than it warrants and "put himself into a passion, unconsciously, for the sake of reinvigorating himself"?

3 Some sports are highly competitive; others depend on co-operation; others consist of isolated activity. Do the conclusions put forward here help to explain why you prefer certain sports to others?

4 Should our knowledge of such bodily changes as these lead us to the gloomy conclusion that "man is at the mercy of his chemistry"? How can such knowledge be misused?

AT THE risk of digression from my main theme, I must here give a warning. In a period of history which might be known as the age of the common man, the individual is being overwhelmed by organization. Around the social relationship, many quite proper interests such as economic and social studies have grown. Other interests are, whatever is said to the contrary, capable of abuse. Every society has to develop rules for the convenience of its members, but when men are reduced, as they often are by personnel management however disguised by arrogant talk of welfare, to indifferent and mediocre servitors of panoptical factories, then the duty of medicine, and I hope of other charitable disciplines, is to oppose.

Medicine is part of the philosophy of life; it is not a social service. Medicine is solely concerned that in the vortex of social relations the individual human personality in every manifestation of living and being is not only preserved intact but flourishes. Curiously, many who in other connections speak of totality of response or the total situation, are prepared to divide human beings into physical, mental, and even spiritual segments. I will have none of this. Men, like health, are catholic and indivisible. I suggest that social medicine is the study and nurture of the human personality in and as part of interpersonal relationships. Definitions are useful only as conceptual scaffoldings; at least, to my mind, the definition I have suggested is precise and sufficiently delineated to have meaning. Many better will I am sure be offered. . . .

All human beings are the victims of their genetic inheritance which may show itself in blood groups, somatotypes or temperamental traits and in many other ways. The whole personality builds up to needs which result in actions; a successful personality reduces physical and psychological tension by action (Murray and Kluckholn 1948). The reduction of tension, one of the tests of a successful personality, may or may not be possible for any individual within the modern pattern of socially enforced value-orientation standards. As work is more and more organized around the machine, so social uniformity is more and more enforced. The machine is the means of higher standards of living and as such is to be welcomed; its danger is the sociological patterns built around it. Action needs such as hunger are not satisfied physiologically when the factory whistle blows.

Within the social setting man seems forever to be frustrated and dissatisfied. The problem is how men may find freedom to express their personalities with delicacy and decency within the security offered by society. The great enigma is that men are prepared to die for what makes life worth living. Science may tell of knowledge but art tells of value. The thousand million ramifications of detail which makes up a human life are, as Bosanquet (1912) in the Gifford lectures for 1911 says, the expression of an infinitely delicate logic. "Art is, in structure, logic in excelsis" (Temple 1923). The precision of a great artist reveals with exquisite analysis the mystical inspiration of life. The justification of industrial societies is not that they increase material prosperity but permit sufficient differentiation of function to allow the full pursuit of art. Many have failed singularly in this; at best life is judged in humanistic terms. Earlier and more primitive societies did not make this mistake; a large slave or near-slave population supported a small elite, composed of priests and artists representing the ecclesiastical and secular form of intuitive thinking, so that culture at its best was made freely available to all.

Very rapidly, the knowledge of how to prevent pestilence and famine, of how to relieve pain and suffering, is spreading across the world. The ideal man, of perfect physique with a psyche well adjusted according to whichever school of psychoanalysis he favours, unharmed by disease throughout his life which ends only because his mechanism decays, is not a too fantastic picture. All that is good but, just because it is good, life becomes a tragedy. Men do not yet love their neighbour nor are they likely to so long as expression of personality is sought amid the constraints imposed by society. Men, as it were, imprison themselves in each other. Within their social prison, all men can do is to search for happiness. But, "there is no joy in happiness" (Ustinov 1953) and equally "Your joy is your sorrow unmasked" (Gibran 1945). The restless colour of Van Gogh, the crowded angels of Goya, the prisons of Piranesi, the strivings of Picasso and the poems of Francis Thompson were not born of happiness. If health includes freedom from pain and anguish then St. John of the Cross was unhealthy. More than any other person, St. John understood the value of life. Health has little to do with freedom from hunger, pain or unhappiness so feared by men. Suffering and anguish may, as the saints have found, be the most precious gifts, which, with the imperious urge of the artist, give to man, albeit for a fragmentary and momentary particle of Newtonian time, a gloriously fulfilling glimpse of the reality beyond this world. Only thus can the value and meaning of human being and living be but dimly understood. Maybe, health is only reached in death. The ineffable but neotic joy of Divine Grace is the prevenient requisite of health. Quite simply, health is understanding—and for this reason, is so seldom, if ever, given to men.

From "Medicine, Society, and Health" by T. A. Lloyd Davies

1 What justification is there for saying "the individual is being overwhelmed by organization"? What are the chief restraints on your freedom to express your individuality? What are the chief opportunities for such expression, and how have these opportunities been brought about?

2 What do you consider to be the purpose of medicine?

3 "A successful personality reduces physical and psychological tension by action." What other abilities or attributes do you expect "a successful personality" to have?

4 What did Ustinov mean by the apparent paradox "there is no joy in happiness"?

5 What does the motto "Industry the servant of art" imply?

6 The first two passages were about the *nature* of man's being. What aspect of man's being does this passage concentrate on?

THE INGESTION of LSD, mescaline or psilocybin can produce a wide range of subjective and objective effects. The subjective effects apparently depend on at least three kinds of variable : the properties and potency of the drug itself; the basic personality traits and current mood of the person ingesting it, and the social and psychological context, including the meaning to the individual of his act in taking the drug and his interpretation of the motives of those who made it available. The discussion of subjective effects that follows is compiled from many different accounts of the drug experience; it should be considered an inventory of possible effects rather than a description of a typical episode.

One subjective experience that is frequently reported is a change in visual perception. When the eyes are open, the perception of light and space is affected : colours become more vivid and seem to glow; the space between objects becomes more apparent, as though space itself had become "real", and surface details appear to be more sharply defined. Many people feel a new awareness of the physical beauty of the world, particularly of visual harmonies, colours, the play of light and the exquisiteness of detail.

The visual effects are even more striking when the eyes are closed. A constantly changing display appears, its content ranging from abstract forms to dramatic scenes involving imagined people or animals, sometimes in exotic lands or ancient times. Different individuals have recalled seeing wavy lines, cobweb or chessboard designs, gratings, mosaics, carpets, floral designs, gems, windmills, mausoleums, landscapes, "arabesques spiralling into eternity", statuesque men of the past, chariots, sequences of dramatic action, the face of Buddha, the face of Christ, the Crucifixion, "the mythical dwelling places of the gods", the immensity and blackness of space. After taking peyote Silas Weir Mitchell wrote : "To give the faintest idea of the perfectly satisfying intensity and purity of these gorgeous coloured fruits is quite beyond my power." A painter described the waning hours of the effects of psilocybin as follows : "As the afternoon wore on I felt very content to simply sit and stare out of the window at the snow and the trees, and at that time I recall feeling that the snow, the fire in the fireplace, the darkened and book-lined room were so perfect as to seem almost unreal."

The changes in visual perception are not always pleasant. Aldous Huxley called one of his books about mescaline Heaven and Hell in recognition of the contradictory sensations induced by the drug. The "hellish" experiences include an impression of blackness accompanied by feelings of gloom and isolation, a garish modification of the glowing colours observed in the "heavenly" phase, a sense of sickly greens and ugly dark reds. The subject's perception of his own body may become unpleasant : his limbs may seem to be distorted or his flesh to be decaying; in a mirror his face may appear to be a mask, his smile a meaningless grimace. Sometimes all human movements appear to be mere puppetry, or everyone seems to be dead. These experiences can be so disturbing that a residue of fear and depression persists long after the effects of the drug have worn off.

Often there are complex auditory hallucinations as well as visual ones : lengthy conversations between imaginary people, perfectly orchestrated musical compositions the subject has never heard before, voices speaking foreign languages unknown to the subject. There have also been reports of hallucinatory odours and tastes and of visceral and other bodily sensations. Frequently patterns of association normally confined to a single sense will cross over to other senses : the sound of music evokes the visual impression of jets of coloured light, a "cold" human voice makes the subject shiver, pricking the skin with a pin produces the visual impression of a circle, light glinting on a Christmas tree ornament seems to shatter and to evoke the sound of sleigh bells. The time sense is altered too. The passage of time may seem to be a slow and pleasant flow or to be intolerably tedious. A "sense of timelessness" is often reported; the subject feels outside of or beyond time, or time and space seem infinite.

In some individuals one of the most basic constancies in perception is affected: the distinction between subject and object. A firm sense of personal identity depends on knowing accurately the borders of the self and on being able to distinguish what is inside from what is outside. Paranoia is the most vivid pathological instance of the breakdown of this discrimination; the paranoiac attributes to personal and impersonal forces outside himself the impulses that actually are inside him. Mystical and transcendental experiences are marked by the loss of this same basic constancy. "All is one" is the prototype of a mystical utterance. In the mystical state the distinction between subject and object disappears; the subject is seen to be one with the object. The experience is usually one of rapture or ecstasy and in religious terms is described as "holy". When the subject thus achieves complete identification with the object, the experience seems beyond words.

From "The Hallucinogenic Drugs" by
F. Barron, M. E. Jarvik, and S. Bunnell, Jr.
Copyright © 1964 by <i>Scientific American</i>, Inc. All rights reserved

1   What meaning would you attach to the pleasant and unpleasant sensations that LSD induces? Is drug-induced happiness or wonder less "real" than other happiness or wonder? If so, why?

2   Is there any difference between the action and effects of the hallucinogenic drugs here mentioned and "too much beer"? In what respects does the habit of drinking beer differ from the habit of taking drugs?

3   Has a man the right to take drugs if he wants to? Any kind of drug? In all circumstances?

4   If chemicals can so stimulate our "patterns of association", why do not artists and scientists resort to them more often for inspiration?

5   Are the scientists about to explain away all mystical and transcendental experience? What about the "suffering and anguish" mentioned in the previous extract? Or do such states and emotions merely produce the requisite chemical changes in the body? Would it be possible to test such a hypothesis?

6   Should society enforce controls over the taking of *all* drugs? If so, what controls? How could they be enforced?

"THERE'S NO occasion for Mr. Pickwick to move, Mr. Perker," said Fogg, untying the red tape which encircled the little bundle, and smiling again more sweetly than before. "Mr. Pickwick is pretty well acquainted with these proceedings. There are no secrets between us, I think. He! he! he!"

"Not many, I think," said Dodson. "Ha! ha! ha!" Then both the partners laughed together, pleasantly and cheerfully, as men who are going to receive money often do.

"We shall make Mr. Pickwick pay for peeping," said Fogg, with considerable native humour, as he unfolded his papers. "The amount of the taxed costs is one hundred and thirty-three, six, four, Mr. Perker."

There was a great comparing of papers and turning over of leaves by Fogg and Perker after this statement of profit and loss, during which Dodson said in an affable manner to Mr. Pickwick,—

"I don't think you are looking quite as stout as when I had the pleasure of seeing you last, Mr. Pickwick."

"Possibly not, sir," replied Mr. Pickwick, who had been flashing forth looks of fierce indignation, without producing the smallest effect on either of the sharp practitioners; "I believe I am not, sir. I have been persecuted and annoyed by scoundrels of late, sir." Perker coughed violently, and asked Mr. Pickwick whether he wouldn't like to look at the morning paper. To which inquiry Mr. Pickwick returned a most decided negative.

"True," said Dodson, "I daresay you have been annoyed in the Fleet; there are some odd gentry there. Whereabouts were your apartments, Mr. Pickwick?"

"My one room," replied that much-injured gentleman, "was on the Coffee Room flight."

"Oh, indeed!" said Dodson. "I believe that is a very pleasant part of the establishment."

"Very," replied Mr. Pickwick dryly.

There was a coolness about all this which to a gentleman of an excitable temperament had, under the circumstances, rather an exasperating tendency. Mr. Pickwick restrained his wrath by gigantic efforts; but when Perker wrote a cheque for the whole amount, and Fogg deposited it in a small pocket-book with a triumphant smile playing over his pimply features, which communicated itself likewise to the stern countenance of Dodson, he felt the blood in his cheeks tingling with indignation.

"Now, Mr. Dodson," said Fogg, putting up the pocket-book and drawing on his gloves, "I am at your service." "Very good," said Dodson, rising, "I am quite ready." "I am very happy," said Fogg, softened by the cheque, "to have had the pleasure of making Mr.

Pickwick's acquaintance. I hope you don't think quite so badly of us, Mr. Pickwick, as when we first had the pleasure of seeing you."

"I hope not," said Dodson, with the high tone of calumniated virtue. "Mr. Pickwick now knows us better, I trust. Whatever your opinion of gentlemen of our profession may be, I beg to assure you, sir, that I bear no ill-will or vindictive feeling towards you for the sentiments you thought proper to express in our office in Freeman's Court, Cornhill, on the occasion to which my partner has referred."

"Oh, no, no, nor I," said Fogg, in a most forgiving manner.

"Our conduct, sir," said Dodson, "will speak for itself, and justify itself, I hope, upon every occasion. We have been in the profession some years, Mr. Pickwick, and have been honoured with the confidence of many excellent clients. I wish you good-morning, sir."

"Good-morning, Mr. Pickwick," said Fogg. So saying, he put his umbrella under his arm, drew off his right glove, and extended the hand of reconciliation to that most indignant gentleman, who thereupon thrust his hands beneath his coat tails, and eyed the attorney with looks of scornful amazement.

"Lowten!" cried Perker at this moment, "open the door."

"Wait one instant," said Mr. Pickwick. "Perker, I will speak."

"My dear sir, pray let the matter rest where it is," said the little attorney, who had been in a state of nervous apprehension during the whole interview; "Mr. Pickwick, I beg —"

"I will not be put down, sir," replied Mr. Pickwick, hastily. — "Mr. Dodson, you have addressed some remarks to me."

Dodson turned round, bent his head meekly, and smiled.

"Some remarks to me," repeated Mr. Pickwick, almost breathless; "and your partner has tendered me his hand, and you have both assumed a tone of forgiveness and highmindedness which is an extent of impudence that I was not prepared for, even in you."

"What, sir!" exclaimed Dodson.

"What, sir!" reiterated Fogg.

"Do you know that I have been the victim of your plots and conspiracies?" continued Mr. Pickwick. "Do you know that I am the man whom you have been imprisoning and robbing? Do you know that you were the attorneys for the plaintiff, in Bardell and Pickwick?"

"Yes, sir, we do know it," replied Dodson.

"Of course we know it, sir," rejoined Fogg, slapping his pocket, perhaps by accident.

"I see that you recollect it with satisfaction," said Mr. Pickwick, attempting to call up a sneer for the first time in his life, and failing most signally in so doing. "Although I have long been anxious to tell you, in plain terms, what my opinion of you is, I should have let even this opportunity pass, in deference to my friend Perker's wishes, but for the unwarrantable tone you have assumed and your insolent familiarity. I say insolent familiarity, sir," said Mr. Pickwick, turning upon Fogg with a fierceness of gesture which caused that person to retreat towards the door with great expedition.

"Take care, sir," said Dodson, who although he was the biggest man of the party, had prudently intrenched himself behind Fogg, and was speaking over his head with a very pale face.— "Let him assault you, Mr. Fogg; don't return it on any account."

"No, no, I won't return it," said Fogg, falling back a little more as he spoke, to the evident relief of his partner, who by these means was gradually getting into the outer office.

"You are," continued Mr. Pickwick, resuming the thread of his discourse — "you are a well-matched pair of mean, rascally, pettifogging robbers."

"Well," interposed Perker, "is that all?"

"It is all summed up in that," rejoined Mr. Pickwick; "they are mean, rascally, pettifogging robbers."

"There!" said Perker, in a most conciliatory tone. "My dear sirs, he has said all he has to say. Now pray go. — Lowten, is that door open?"

Mr. Lowten, with a distant giggle, replied in the affirmative.

"There, there — good-morning — good-morning — now pray, my dear sirs — Mr. Lowten, the door!" cried the little man, pushing Dodson and Fogg, nothing loth, out of the office; "this way, my dear sirs — now pray don't prolong this — dear me — Mr. Lowten — the door, sir — why don't you attend?"

"If there's law in England, sir," said Dodson, looking towards Mr. Pickwick, as he put on his hat, "you shall smart for this."

"You are a couple of mean —"

"Remember, sir, you pay dearly for this," said Fogg.

"—Rascally, pettifogging robbers!" continued Mr. Pickwick, taking not the least notice of the threats that were addressed to him

"Robbers!" cried Mr. Pickwick, running to the stairhead, as the two attorneys descended.

"Robbers!" shouted Mr. Pickwick, breaking from Lowten and Perker, and thrusting his head out of the staircase window.

When Mr. Pickwick drew in his head again, his countenance was smiling and placid; and walking quietly back into the office, he declared that he had now removed a great weight from his mind, and that he felt perfectly comfortable and happy.

From *The Pickwick Papers* by Charles Dickens

1 Mr. Pickwick is livid with anger one minute, smiling and placid the next. Why should the repetition of a few opprobrious words effect such a change in him?

2 What factors play the biggest part in the fashioning of a person's temperament? In what ways are a person's character, his temperament, and his personality different, and in what respects are they interdependent?

3 Mr. Pickwick, who was usually a very good humoured and cheerful person, found it difficult to express his anger openly, but felt greatly relieved when he had done so. Do you think it is desirable to express anger on occasions or do you believe that it is better to hide it? What uses do you see for anger?

4 "Though we strive always to be more charitable, patient, generous and tolerant; though we give fewer and fewer causes for offence: yet is just as much offence taken." Is the appetite for being offended a constant in some temperaments?

I RESOLVED in my future conduct to redeem the past; and I can say with honesty that my resolve was fruitful of some good. You know yourself how earnestly in the last months of last year I laboured to relieve suffering; you know that much was done for others, and that the days passed quietly, almost happily for myself. Nor can I truly say that I wearied of this beneficent and innocent life; I think instead that I daily enjoyed it more completely; but I was still cursed with my duality of purpose; and as the first edge of my penitence wore off, the lower side of me, so long indulged, so recently chained down, began to growl for license. Not that I dreamed of resuscitating Hyde; the bare idea of that would startle me to frenzy: no, it was in my own person that I was once more tempted to trifle with my conscience; and it was as an ordinary secret sinner that I at last fell before the assaults of temptation.

There comes an end to all things; the most capacious measure is filled at last; and this brief condescension to my evil finally destroyed the balance of my soul. And yet I was not alarmed; the fall seemed natural, like a return to the old days before I had made my discovery. It was a fine, clear January day, wet under foot where the frost had melted, but cloudless overhead; and the Regent's Park was full of winter chirrupings and sweet with spring odours. I sat in the sun on a bench; the animal within me licking the chops of memory; the spiritual side a little drowsed, promising subsequent penitence, but not yet moved to begin. After all, I reflected, I was like my neighbours; and then I smiled, comparing myself with other men, comparing my active good-will with the lazy cruelty of their neglect. And at the very moment of that vainglorious thought, a qualm came over me, a horrid nausea and the most deadly shuddering. These passed away, and left me faint; and then as in its turn the faintness subsided, I began to be aware of a change in the temper of my thoughts, a greater boldness, a contempt of danger, a solution of the bonds of obligation. I looked down; my clothes hung formlessly on my shrunken limbs; the hand that lay on my knee was corded and hairy. I was once more Edward Hyde. A moment before I had been safe of all men's respect, wealthy, beloved—the cloth laying for me in the dining-room at home; and now I was the common quarry of mankind, hunted, houseless, a known murderer, thrall to the gallows. . . .

When I came to myself at Lanyon's, the horror of my old friend perhaps affected me somewhat : I do not know; it was at least but a drop in the sea to the abhorrence with which I looked back upon these hours. A change had come over me. It was no longer the fear of the gallows, it was the horror of being Hyde that racked me. I received Lanyon's condemnation partly in a dream; it was partly in a dream that I came home to my own house and got into bed. I slept after the prostration of the day, with a stringent and profound slumber which not even the nightmares that wrung me could avail to break. I awoke in the morning shaken, weakened, but refreshed. I still hated and feared the thought of the brute that slept within me, and I had not of course forgotten the appalling dangers of the day before; but I was once more at home, in my own house and close to my drugs; and gratitude for my escape shone so strong in my soul that it almost rivalled the brightness of hope.

I was stepping leisurely across the court after breakfast, drinking the chill of the air with pleasure, when I was seized again with those indescribable sensations that heralded the change; and I had but the time to gain the shelter of my cabinet, before I was once again raging and freezing with the passions of Hyde. It took on this occasion a double dose to recall me to myself; and, alas! six hours after, as I sat sadly looking into the fire, the pangs returned, and the drug had to be re-administered. In short, from that day forth it seemed only by a great effort as of gymnastics, and only under the immediate stimulation of the drug, that I was able to wear the countenance of Jekyll. At all hours of the day and night I would be taken with the premonitory shudder; above all, if I slept, or even dozed for a moment in my chair, it was always as Hyde that I awakened. . . .

It is useless, and the time awfully fails me, to prolong this description; no one has ever suffered such torments, let that suffice; and yet even to these, habit brought—no, not alleviation—but a certain callousness of soul, a certain acquiescence of despair; and my punishment might have gone on for years, but for the last calamity which has now fallen, and which has finally severed me from my own face and nature. My provision of the salt, which had never been renewed since the date of the first experiment, began to run low. I sent out for a fresh supply, and mixed the draught; the ebullition followed, and the first change of colour, not the second; I drank it, and it was without efficiency. You will learn from Poole how I have had London ransacked; it was in vain; and I am now persuaded that my first supply was impure, and that it was that unknown impurity which lent efficacy to the draught.

About a week has passed, and I am now finishing this statement under the influence of the last of the old powders. This then, is the last time, short of a miracle, that Henry Jekyll can think his own thoughts or see his own face (now how sadly altered!) in the glass.

From *The Strange Case of Dr. Jekyll and Mr. Hyde*
by R. L. Stevenson

1 "The non-criminal is the man who has learned to control his criminality." Do you agree that man is compounded of love and hate, good and evil, and that only intensive education and social indoctrination enable him to behave in a civilized manner? Do you believe that a murderer should be regarded as a person to be punished or a person to be healed?

2 Bearing in mind the example of the Hitler Youth and of the children in Orwell's *1984*, what criteria for that education and social indoctrination previously mentioned are necessary if civilized man is to survive?

3 Reformers urge that more of the mentally ill should be treated at home. Other reformers urge the extension of probation in the treatment of criminal offenders. Argue the case for and against the treatment of an individual breakdown in its normal social milieu.

4 Consider the concept of conscience. *Should* conscience give free rein to vicious imaginings? *Can* it restrain them?

5 What do you understand by the term "free will"? How might it apply to the following alternatives with regard to one's neighbour's wife?
   (i) To desire her and let time pass.
   (ii) To suppress desire of her.
   (iii) To desire her and avoid her.
   (iv) To desire her and seduce her.
   Is it fallacious to regard such decisions as being entirely the responsibility of the individual?

6 Can man be immoral to himself, or does morality only exist in terms of man's relationships with and behaviour towards others?

Part Two

The Need to Relate

AFTER BREAKFAST Levin was not in the same place in the string of mowers as before, but found himself between the old man who had accosted him quizzically, and now invited him to be his neighbour, and a young peasant who had only been married in the autumn and who was mowing this summer for the first time.

The old man, holding himself erect, went in front, moving with long, regular strides, his feet turned out and swinging his scythe as precisely and evenly, and apparently as effortlessly, as a man swings his arms in walking. As if it were child's play, he laid the grass in a high, level ridge. It seemed as if the sharp blade swished of its own accord through the juicy grass.

Behind Levin came the lad Mishka. His pleasant, boyish face, with a twist of fresh grass bound round his hair, worked all the time with effort; but whenever anyone looked at him he smiled. He would clearly sooner die than own it was hard work for him.

Levin kept between them. In the very heat of the day the mowing did not seem such hard work. The perspiration with which he was drenched cooled him, while the sun, that burned his back, his head, and his arms, bare to the elbow, gave a vigour and dogged energy to his labour; and more and more often now came those moments of oblivion, when it was possible not to think of what one was doing. The scythe cut of itself. Those were happy moments. Still more delightful were the moments when they reached the river at the end of the rows and the old man would rub his scythe with a thick knot of wet grass, rinse the steel blade in the fresh water of the stream, ladle out a little in a tin dipper and offer Levin a drink.

"What do you say to my home-brew, eh? Good, eh?" he would say with a wink.

And truly Levin had never tasted any drink so good as this warm water with bits of grass floating in it and a rusty flavour from the tin dipper. And immediately after this came the blissful, slow saunter, with his hand on the scythe, during which he could wipe away the streaming sweat, fill his lungs with air, and look about at the long line of mowers and at what was happening around in the forest and the country.

The longer Levin mowed, the oftener he experienced those moments of oblivion when it was not his arms which swung the scythe but the scythe seemed to mow of itself, a body full of life and consciousness of its own, and as though by magic, without a thought being given to it, the work did itself regularly and carefully. These were the most blessed moments. . . .

Levin did not notice how time was passing. Had he been asked how long he had been working he would have answered, "Half an hour"— and it was getting on for dinner-time. As they were walking back over the cut grass, the old man drew Levin's attention to the little girls and boys approaching from different sides, along the road and through the long grass—hardly visible above it—carrying the haymakers' pitchers of rye-beer stoppered with rags, and bundles of bread which dragged their little arms down.

"Look'ee, little lady-birds crawling along!" he said, pointing to them and glancing at the sun from under his hand.

They completed two more rows; the old man stopped.

"Come, master, dinner-time!" he said briskly. And on reaching the stream the mowers moved across the cut grass towards their pile of coats, where the children who had brought their dinners sat waiting for them. The men who had driven from a distance gathered in the shadow of their carts; those who lived nearer went under a willow bush, over which they threw grass.

Levin sat down beside them; he did not want to go away.

All constraint in the presence of the master had disappeared long ago. The peasants began preparing for dinner. Some had a wash, the young lads bathed in the stream, others arranged places for their after-dinner rest, untied their bundles of bread and unstoppered their pitchers of rye-beer.

The old man crumbled up some bread in a cup, pounded it with the handle of a spoon, poured water on it from the dipper, broke up some more bread and, having sprinkled it with salt, turned to the east to say his prayer.

"Come, master, have some of my dinner," he said, squatting on his knees in front of the cup.

The bread and water was so delicious that Levin changed his mind about going home. He shared the old man's meal and chatted to him about his family affairs, taking the keenest interest in them, and told him about his own affairs and all the circumstances that could be of interest to the old peasant. He felt much nearer to him than to his brother, and could not help smiling at the affection he felt for this man. When the old chap got up again, said his prayer, and lay down under a bush, putting some grass under his head for a pillow, Levin did the same and, in spite of the clinging flies that were so persistent in the sunshine and the insects that tickled his hot face and body, he fell asleep at once, and only woke when the sun had gone the other side of the bush and reached him. The old man had been awake some time and sat whetting the scythes of the younger lads

Levin looked about him and hardly recognized the place, everything was so altered. A wide expanse of meadow was already mown and the sweet-smelling hay shone with a peculiar fresh glitter in the slanting rays of the evening sun. And the bushes by the river had been cut down, and the river itself, not visible before, its curves now gleaming like steel, and the peasants getting up and moving about, the steep wall of yet uncut grass, and the hawks hovering over the stripped meadow—all was completely new.

From *Anna Karenina*
by Leo Tolstoy (trans. Rosemary Edmunds)

1   What are the differences, if any, between the labour of the peasant in a string of mowers and the labour of the car factory worker who puts in the front passenger seat as each car comes along the assembly line?

2   People often "forget themselves" during dancing or when drunk. Why should they seek to forget themselves? Can you differentiate between their experiences, according to the way they arrive at this kind of oblivion?

3   Why did Levin, the master, and the old man get on so well together this day? Did they talk about important matters? Was their conversation important? What new roles did they assume, and why?

4   Can you account for Levin's enjoyment of his strenuous exertions, his simple food, his wonder at what he saw when he woke up? Are there any parallels in your own experience? Or does this passage cruelly romanticize labour? At what other times might one experience similar "blessed moments"?

5   We are constantly being warned that leisure must replace work as the arena of achievement for man. Will leisure activities offer more or fewer opportunities for the social cohesion that work has usually conferred? Will they satisfy in the sense that Levin's labours in the field satisfied him?

AFTER THE ten o'clock turnout of public houses Canning Circus gave in to its curfew and became silent. Late cars changed gear as they ascended the hill, showed their dark snouts upon circling the island at the top, then disappeared into the oblivion of an opposite road. A moon illuminated the island's flowerless garden, and the junction's green lamp poles were dimly lighted in comparison to such lunar brilliance.

Arthur and Fred walked by the almshouses talking about war, Fred gesticulating as he threw out his opinions on tactics, fluently comparing Korea to Libya, mountain to desert, "human seas" to tanks. A light shone from a public house in which people were still washing-up. All other doorways and buildings stood empty, their windows darkened by blinds. A few people were about, one man stalking along in the shadows, and another walking boldly across the island whistling the latest song hit. A third person came unsteadily out of the public house clutching a glass beer mug. "See that?" Arthur said, pointing to him. "What's that funny sod doin'?"

Fred saw only an interruption to his flow of speech, but on drawing closer heard the man humming an unrecognizable tune, as if to disguise the purpose of his expedition across the road. He stepped on to the pavement and looked intently into the window of an undertaker's shop.

"I wonder what he's up to?" Arthur repeated.

Having made up his mind, the man took three calculated strides back to the pavement edge and threw the beer mug with great force at the window. The smash sounded musical and carefree, and glass splashed on to the pavement, while the man adroitly dodged the chaos he had caused.

Arthur was stirred by the sound of breaking glass: it synthesized all the anarchism within him, was the most perfect and suitable noise to accompany the end of the world and himself. He ran towards the disturbance, each strike of his boots on the pavement sending an echo through the empty circle of buildings, rebounding from each deserted corner.

"Come on," he called to Fred.

Several people already stood near the undertaker's window, as if they had sprung out of the ground, and by the doorway a woman held the bewildered culprit by his wrist. Arthur peered closer and saw that another woman, younger and wearing an Army uniform the colour of which immediately prejudiced him, had taken command, and had sent someone to fetch the police. Fred grinned at the jagged hole, at giant cracks running away from it in all directions, at headstones, scrolls, and earthen flower vases splattered with glass. He laughed at the wreck, and pushed some glass into the gutter with his shoe cap.

"What's up, missis?" a raincoated pipesmoker wanted to know. "What's 'e done?" nodding at the man held by the wrist, who grinned with great friendliness at each new arrival.

"Chucked a pint jar at that window," Arthur said.

"He did that," the woman in khaki told him, pointing at the wrecked window like a museum guide showing off a prize exhibit. She was a woman of about thirty-five, her prominent bosom emphasized by highly polished buttons. Arthur noted her thin lips, high cheekbones, eyes that did not open very wide, a low forehead, and hair that just curled out of the back of her peaked cap and rested on her shaved neck. Weighing her up, he wondered if she had ever been loved. He doubted it. She was the sort of woman who would spit in a man's eye if he tried to be nice to her, though at the same time he supposed her to be the sort who wanted most of all in the world to be loved. Only you could tell by her face that she would kick you if you tried. Old Rat Face, he said to himself, that's what she is. Potatoes and Horsemeat.

"She's a fawce bogger," a man said, half in admiration, half in contempt. "She knows what she's doing right enough."

"You'll get a stripe for this," Arthur cried. "Right across your back."

Most of the interest was focused on him, standing mutely by the woman who held his limp and resistless wrist. He was neither young nor middle-aged, a man who seemed to have a stake in two generations without being cradled and carried along by either one. His face seemed marked by some years of marriage, yet this branded him as a single man, an odd, lonely person who gave off an air of belonging nowhere at all, which caused Arthur to think him half witted. The uniformed woman looked as though she also had never had a home and belonged nowhere, but she had aligned herself with order and law, and sympathy was against her. The man turned slightly towards the window. He had brown hair that receded over a narrow forehead, and his pink face looked as though it had just been thoroughly washed. With the arm that was not held, he pointed through the glass to a black flower vase covered by a metal grid, and to the grey, partly inscribed headstone. In Loving Memory Of.

"I only wanted one o' them," he said, looking around for approval, "and one o' these." He spoke with a whine, as though he really meant to smash the window, and that for this reason he should eventually be released by the elder woman at his side.

"Why did you do such a barmy thing, mate?" Arthur called out. "That winder worn't worth smashin'."

He looked at him as if he brought some hope, and pointed again at the two objects. "I wanted that there," he said with simple insistence.

Sympathetic voices gave him confidence, and while he still hoped for some sort of release, seemed pleased that he saw such an attraction. From the look in his eyes and the grin on his face, it was as though he might be dreaming or did not quite believe where he was, or that the situation was some kind of game. "I wanted them things for my mother," inclining his head again to the window. The tone of his voice indicated that he should continue, but he stopped speaking, as if only capable of making one sentence at a time, and in a moment of excitement he had thought to stray beyond this line.

"Let's go off home," Fred suggested. "Them owd 'ags'll 'and 'im over to the coppers. There's nowt ter wait for."

Arthur preferred to stay, standing with a blank mind, as if he were at the theatre watching a play, fascinated but unable to participate.

"Where's your mother then?" several people called out at once.
The woman in khaki braced herself. "Leave him alone. The police
will ask him all the questions. He can do all his talking to them."
Some wit from the crowd asked him again where his mother was, and
he turned to them with a grave look, saying solemnly : "I buried her
three months ago. I didn't mean no harm missis," he said gently to
the woman holding him.

"All the same," she said, "you didn't need to do this."

A woman called out that the police were coming. Fred edged closer
to the prisoner. "You was daft to do that," he said, in a voice that
precluded either hope or assistance.

"There are bigger and better winders ter smash down-town,"
Arthur said. "I know a clinker on Long Row, wi' furniture behind it!"

"I wanted it for my mother. I've only just buried her."

"You'll get six months in Lincoln for this," someone from the back
shouted, showing a dual knowledge of geography and justice that
made everybody laugh. The woman holding him asked them to be
quiet and leave him alone : their taunts made him nervous.

"Let me go, missis," he said to her secretively, as if her plea meant
that she was now on his side. "Go on, be a sport. I didn't mean no
harm. I'd on'y had a pint or two."

The woman in khaki turned on him sharply. "Shut up, you. You'll
stay where you are and wait for the police."

"Ark at 'er," somebody said. "She talks to 'im as if 'e was dirt, the
poor bogger."

A new wave of curiosity caught every member of the crowd at the
same time, and interest moved to the vital statistics of the man
himself. They asked where he lived, how many kids he had, where he
worked, what was his name, and how old he was. But so many questions
confused him, and he could not answer. In a loud voice the woman
in khaki told them to leave the questions for the police, as though
her only function on earth was to live until they came.

He still looked for salvation from the woman by his side. "Let me
off, missis, please," he said. "Be a sport." She held him so loosely
that it did not occur to him to snap his wrist free and run. Such a
thought had been in Arthur's mind for some time. "Why don't you
run mate?" he whispered. "You'll be all right. I wain't stop yer and
my brother wain't."

"Don't put ideas into his head," the Army woman barked. "You
shut yer bleedin' rattle Rat Face," he said contemptuously. "You
want a good pastin'. What good will it do you to hand him over to
the coppers? Your sort won't let a bloke live. Just walk off," he called
to the man. "Rat Face won't stop you."

The man had so many allies that he looked at each new voice as it piped up, a radiant grin never leaving him, even when he again mentioned the fact that he hadn't long ago buried his mother. The crowd began shouting that he be set free but, standing with her legs slightly apart, the woman in khaki held her ground. Arthur passed him a lighted cigarette, placing it between his trembling fingers. "Run!" he whispered.

"I couldn't," he said, puffing nervously, "this woman won't let me."

"She ain't got owt to do wi' it," he argued. "Get crackin' an' run." A gangway opened through which he could escape. "They'll shove you in clink," Arthur said, "and no mistake."

Panic overspread his face, and with a sudden movement he snapped his wrist free.

"Stay where you are!" Rat Face ordered.

He looked around, bewildered, not knowing what to do, unable to force the ratchet-claws of the trap from his brain. Arthur stood on the doorway so as not to obstruct his escape. Quick decision entered into all lines of the man's face at once, and the grin that it had worn for so long left it like the flick of a shutter.

Rat Face attempted to hold him. She caught him by the arm but he pushed her roughly away. She tried to slap him but he held her wrist and twisted it, and encouragement from the crowd gave him strength to break finally from her grip. He stood trembling, ready to sprint clear of them.

As suddenly as his way of escape opened, the crowd for some reason closed their ranks. Hope never left a human face more quickly. A police officer stood facing him.

Questions were answered truthfully, briefly, and with alacrity, as if the man had been asked the same ones many times before, and as if he was now relieved that he did not have to make the decision whether or not to run away. He enjoyed giving the answers, as if his salvation lay in appearing pleased to do so, and in his smile was an all-embracing desire to satisfy the police with their clarity, and amuse the now silent crowd by their contents. The two women who held him made their statements.

"Any more of you like to witness?" the policeman said, looking around. No one moved. The squad car with the man inside circled the island and descended towards the city centre by a subsidiary street, its wireless antennae bending backwards and forwards from the sudden movement of starting.

From *Saturday Night and Sunday Morning* by Alan Sillitoe

1 Why did this man smash the window, why did he behave as he did when the crowd gathered, and why was he so helpful to the police? Why did he grin nearly all the time?

2 Why do individual people congregate at the scene of an accident or of violent action? Are they impelled by curiosity, the desire to help, a kind of vindictiveness, or a craving for sensation? What drives them there and what *keeps* them there? Do they get any kind of satisfaction from the experience?

3 "She was the sort of woman who would spit in a man's eye if he tried to be nice to her, though at the same time he supposed her to be the sort who wanted most of all in the world to be loved." Can you explain such apparent perversity in human conduct? Are women more prone to it than men? How can one help such people to enter into and enjoy relationships with others?

4 What is loneliness—a physical situation, an attitude of mind, or a disease? Why has loneliness been described as "the curse of modern urban industrial civilization"? What substitutes for real relationships do lonely people find? How does society try to combat loneliness through its official agencies? Could more be done?

5 Give two first-person accounts of this incident, one from the standpoint of the man who smashed the window, and the other from the standpoint of any of the other participants or onlookers—the woman who held him, the woman in Army uniform, Arthur, Fred, the policeman, or anyone in the crowd.

6 Human beings usually take a long time to "get to know each other". Can some extreme situations or experiences really enable people to get to know each other all at once? Or must we always experience each other's behaviour in a variety of situations before we can claim such knowledge and relationship? Is to know, to love?

7 Why do human beings so need to love and to be loved?

WE WENT a long way, to the bottom of the field, where a wagon stood half-loaded. Festoons of untrimmed grass hung down like curtains all around it. We crawled underneath, between the wheels, into a herb-scented cave of darkness. Rosie scratched about, turned over a sack, and revealed a stone jar of cider.

"It's cider," she said "You ain't to drink it though. Not much of it, any rate."

Huge and squat, the jar lay on the grass like an unexploded bomb. We lifted it up, unscrewed the stopper, and smelt the whiff of fermented apples. I held the jar to my mouth and rolled my eyes sideways, like a beast at a water-hole. "Go on," said Rosie. I took a deep breath. . . .

Never to be forgotten, that first long secret drink of golden fire, juice of those valleys and of that time, wine of wild orchards, of russet summer, of plump red apples, and Rosie's burning cheeks. Never to be forgotten, or ever tasted again. . . .

I put down the jar with a gulp and a gasp. Then I turned to look at Rosie. She was yellow and dusty with buttercups and seemed to be purring in the gloom; her hair was rich as a wild bee's nest and her eyes were full of stings. I did not know what to do about her, nor did I know what not to do. She looked smooth and precious, a thing of unplumbable mysteries, and perilous as quicksand.

"Rosie . . ." I said, on my knees, and shaking.

She crawled with a rustle of grass towards me, quick and superbly assured. Her hand in mine was like a small wet flame which I could neither hold nor throw away. Then Rosie, with a remorseless, reedy strength, pulled me down from my tottering perch, pulled me down, down into her wide green smile and into the deep subaqueous grass.

Then I remember little, and that little, vaguely. Skin drums beat in my head. Rosie was close-up, salty, an invisible touch, too near to be seen or measured. And it seemed that the wagon under which we lay went floating away like a barge, out over the valley where we rocked unseen, swinging on motionless tides.

Then she took off her boots and stuffed them with flowers. She did the same with mine. Her parched voice crackled like flames in my ears. More fires were started. I drank more cider. Rosie told me outrageous fantasies. She liked me, she said, better than Walt, or Ken, Boney Harris, or even the curate. And I admitted to her, in a loud, rough voice, that she was even prettier than Betty Gleed. For a long time we sat with our mouths very close, breathing the same hot air. We kissed, once only, so dry and shy, it was like two leaves colliding in air.

At last the cuckoos stopped singing and slid into the woods. The mowers went home and left us. I heard Jack calling as he went down the lane, calling my name till I heard him no more. And still we lay in our wagon of grass tugging at each other's hands, while her husky, perilous whisper drugged me and the cider beat gongs in my head. . . .

Night came at last, and we crawled out from the wagon and stumbled together towards home. Bright dew and glow-worms shone over the grass, and the heat of the day grew softer. I felt like a giant; I swung from the trees and plunged my arms into nettles just to show her. Whatever I did seemed valiant and easy. Rosie carried her boots and smiled.

There was something about that evening which dilates the memory, even now. The long hills slavered like Chinese dragons, crimson in the setting sun. The shifting lane lassoed my feet and tried to trip me up. And the lake, as we passed it, rose hissing with waves and tried to drown us among its cannibal fish. Perhaps I fell in—though I don't remember. But here I lost Rosie for good. I found myself wandering home alone, wet through, and possessed by miracles. I discovered extraordinary tricks of sight. I could make trees move and leapfrog each other, and turn bushes into roaring trains. I could lick up the stars like acid drops and fall flat on my face without pain. I felt magnificent, fateful, and for the first time in my life, invulnerable to the perils of night.

When at last I reached home, still dripping wet, I was bursting with power and pleasure. I sat on the chopping-block and sang "Fierce Raged the Tempest" and several other hymns of that nature. I went on singing till long after supper-time, bawling alone in the dark. Then Harold and Jack came and frog-marched me to bed. I was never the same again. . . .

From *Cider with Rosie* by Laurie Lee

1   "First love—best love." In what respects?

2   Does nostalgia lend enchantment to our view of certain experiences? Are some experiences unrepeatable? What harms, what benefits stem from our ability to romance?

3   "I was never the same again. . . ." What was the real nature of the author's "transformation"? Can you believe in the delirious force of the experience? Are such transformations always dependent upon another person?

4   Could this experience have been communicated as well by music, or by poem, or by film, as it is in this extract from Laurie Lee's novel? Can you recall other art experiences of like order?

5   Where do you place love between man and woman on the spectrum ranging from romantic ideal to biological urge?

THE BELL doth toll for him that thinks it doth; and though it intermit again, yet from that minute that that occasion wrought upon him, he is united to God. Who casts not up his eye to the sun when it rises? but who takes off his eye from a comet when that breaks out? Who bends not his ear to any bell, which upon any occasion rings? but who can remove it from that bell which is passing a piece of himself out of this world? No man is an island, entire of itself; every man is a piece of the Continent, a part of the main; if a clod be washed away by the sea, Europe is the less, as well as if a promontory were, as well as if a manor of thy friends or of thine own were; any man's death diminishes me, because I am involved in mankind; and therefore never send to know for whom the bell tolls; it tolls for thee.

From *Part of a Sermon* by John Donne

1 Is an intimation of mortality a prerequisite to a knowledge of God? Or does it simply make one think on God more?

2 "Any man's death diminishes me, because I am involved in mankind." An earthquake in Chile, starvation in India, killing in Viet Nam, a landslip in South Wales, a road death at the other end of the street: what perspective of involvement is it possible to have?

3 These words of Donne have been used over and again by social reformers, internationalists, liberals. Are they justified in recruiting the purport of these words to their cause? Is it possible that Donne's intent transcended the apparent meaning?

4 Are we increasing the economic interdependence of men at the expense of personal interdependence? What areas of our thought and being are vitally dependent upon our ability to relate with others?

Part Three

Man in Society

In Tudor times, to strengthen the Royal Prerogative and meet the real needs of that age, there had been a great increase in the number and the power of independent Courts each administering its own legal system with little regard to the procedure and principles of the Common Law. But the Parliaments that opposed James and Charles I, instructed by Edward Coke, the greatest of English lawyers, endeavoured to uphold the supremacy of the Common Law, and in 1641 were able to enforce it by legislation; the Star Chamber, the Ecclesiastical Commission, and the Jurisdiction of the Councils of Wales and of the North were then abolished. The Admiralty Court had already been compelled to accept the control of the Common Law in the development of the important commercial law of England.

Thus the English judicial system escaped the fate of being broken into fragments. The only dualism left was the independence of the Court of Chancery; but even that ceased to be a weapon of Royal Prerogative, and became a complementary system of Judge-made law, ingeniously dovetailed into the principles enforced in the ordinary Courts.

The victory of the Common Law involved the abolition of torture in England long before other countries, and paved the way for a fairer treatment of political enemies of government when brought to trial. Above all, the victory of the Common Law over the Prerogative Courts preserved the medieval conception of the supremacy of law, as a thing that could not be brushed aside for the convenience of government, and could only be altered in full Parliament, not by the King alone. This great principle, that law is above the executive, was indeed violated during the revolutionary period of the Commonwealth and Protectorate. But it re-emerged at the Restoration, and was confirmed at the Revolution of 1688, which was effected against James II precisely to establish the principle that law was above the King. That medieval idea of the supremacy of law as something separate from and independent of the will of the executive, disappeared in continental countries. But in England it became the palladium of our liberties and had a profound effect on English society and habits of thought.

Under the Commonwealth and Protectorate, constitutional law was trodden underfoot in the exigencies of Revolution, but even during that period the Common Law and the lawyers were very strong, strong enough unfortunately to prevent the fulfilment of a loud popular demand for law reform, a crying social need which Cromwell vainly endeavoured to supply. The lawyers were too many for him. Even he was not wholly a dictator : the soldiers on one side, the lawyers on the other, at once supported him and held him in check. When at the Restoration the army was disbanded, the lawyers were left victorious. . . .

Whether or not English justice was on the whole less bad than the continental practice of the day, the philosophers of Europe and of England now began their famous attack on the existing systems of law and punishment. This greater sensitiveness to evils which all previous ages had accepted as matters of course, was part of the general humanitarian movement, connected on the continent with Voltaire and the "philosophers", and in England connected equally with "philosophy" and with religion. The Italian reformer, Beccaria, in his attack on the penal codes of Europe was followed by Howard's on the still scandalous state of prisons at home and abroad, and by Bentham's analysis of the useless and complicated absurdities of English law, a vested interest dear to the heart of the most conservative of professions.

The excellent idea of the rule of law, as something superior to the will of the rulers, was strong among the eighteenth-century English. It had been secured by the events of the Revolution and by the consequent irremovability of Judges, who were no longer jackals of government, but independent umpires between the Crown and the subject.

This high conception of the supremacy of law was popularized by Blackstone's *Commentaries on the Laws of England* (1765), a book widely read by educated people in England and America, for it was a legally-minded age. The fault was that the law thus idealized was regarded too much as static, as a thing given once for all; whereas, if law is indeed to be the permanent rule of life to a nation, it must be apt to change with the changing needs and circumstances of society. In the eighteenth century, Parliament showed little legislative activity, except in private acts for enclosure of land, for turnpike roads, or other economic measures. In administrative matters there was a lag in legislation, at a time when great industrial developments were every year changing social conditions, and adding to the needs of a growing population.

Therefore Jeremy Bentham, the father of English law reform, regarded Blackstone as the arch-enemy, who stood in the way of change by teaching people to make a fetish of the laws of England in the form which they actually bore at the moment, a form dictated by the needs not of the present age but of ages long past.

The first blast against Blackstone was blown by young Bentham in his *Fragment on Government* in 1776, that seminal year which saw the publication of Adam Smith's *Wealth of Nations* the first part of Gibbon's History, and the American Declaration of Independence. When the octogenarian Bentham died in 1832, the laws of England had only just begun to be altered from what they had been when he first denounced them in Blackstone's day. Yet his prolonged efforts had not been in vain, for he had converted the rising generation. Onwards from that time our laws were rapidly changed in accordance with the commonsense, utilitarian principles that Bentham had laid down.

Reform was to be the specific work of the nineteenth century. The specific work of the earlier Hanoverian epoch was the establishment of the rule of law; and that law, with all its grave faults, was at least a law of freedom. On that solid foundation all our subsequent reforms were built. If the eighteenth century had not established the law of freedom, the nineteenth century in England would have proceeded by Revolutionary violence, instead of by Parliamentary modification of the law.

From *English Social History* by G. M. Trevelyan

1 Should the excellence of a country's legal system be judged by its ability to develop so that it can meet the real needs or circumstances of the age?

2 What real needs of *this* age do you think our legal system fails to accommodate?

3 How are such needs to be evaluated, and by whom? What processes will translate such recognition into alteration of the legal system, of the laws, of the penal code?

4 What principles underpin the rule of law? What measures are essential to their safeguard today?

5 Consider some of the differences between the legal system of this country and those of other countries. Do these differences (e.g. the French pre-trial examination of the defendant by the judge) reflect crucial differences of principle, or are they merely administrative variations?

6 What is the relationship between the judiciary, the police, and the legal profession in this country?

7 Consider the advantages and disadvantages of trial by jury.

ONE OF the oldest and best established laws of economics is the proposition in monetary theory known as Gresham's Law. The common formula of this law is: Bad money drives out good. Its more technical formulation, given by H. D. Macleod in 1857, is: The worst form of currency in circulation regulates the value of the whole currency and drives all other forms of currency out of circulation.

On the face of it, this law connects two kinds of social process, neither of which is necessarily brought about by human design: the circulation of an inferior alongside a superior form of currency, and the gradual disappearance from circulation of the superior form. The law is well corroborated. It has been confirmed in a variety of circumstances; where there is underweight or debased coin in circulation with full-weight or pure coin of the same metal; where there are two metals in circulation, and one is undervalued as compared with the other; and where less convertible paper money is put into circulation with a more convertible paper money or with a metallic currency. There are societies to which it does not apply, either because they lack a monetary system, or because their currency is uniform; but if there is any case to which it applies which has falsified it, I at least do not know of it. It is employed in historical explanations; and it has been invoked in making true predictions. Need we say more? . . .

One slight doubt remains. As Popper has taught us, a scientific hypothesis is corroborated, not by accumulating favourable evidence, but by seeking and failing to find unfavourable evidence. Have we truly sought evidence against Gresham's Law? Where might we expect to find it?

Suppose there were a society which had a monetary system, but in which there was little money because each man provided his family's food and shelter by his own labour on his own land; suppose, furthermore, that coins of varying quality circulated side by side, that tendering money was a recognized occasion for display, and that anybody who tendered inferior money was scorned and derided. Anthropologists have encountered societies with practices far more remote from ours than these. What economist would predict that Gresham's Law would be found to hold in such a society?

At this point an objection may be entered. A society such as you have described, it may be protested, does not have a pure monetary system; the tendering of money for goods normally has an object other than to obtain its maximum value in goods, namely, to display the quality of the coins tendered. Now if Gresham's Law is taken to apply only to societies with a pure monetary system, the existence of a society such as I have described cannot falsify it. . . .

That Gresham's Law obtains in a "pure" monetary economy is therefore logically unfalsifiable. Does that dispose of its claim to be a law? After all, do physicists consider Newton's Laws of Motion to be empirically falsifiable?

In mechanics, Newton's Laws of Motion have a special place; indeed if they were abandoned, it would be as reasonable to say that mechanics itself had been abandoned as that it had been revised. And in view of that vast body of knowledge which presupposes mechanics, it is plain that no odd or unexplained phenomenon would tempt any scientist to question the fundamental laws of mechanics itself. . . .

The comparative immunity of Newton's Laws of Motion to empirical falsification is altogether different in character from the logical immunity of Gresham's Law to falsification in a pure monetary system. It would manifestly be trifling to argue that Newton's Laws must hold in any pure mechanical system, if you define a mechanical system in part as one in which Newton's Laws hold. Newton's Laws are laws because it is possible to specify the phenomena for which they hold, without defining those phenomena either in terms of those laws themselves, or in terms of more ultimate laws from which they can be deduced. But it is not possible, so I contend, to specify the phenomena for which Gresham's Law holds, without defining those phenomena in terms of economic laws from which Gresham's Law is deducible. That a given society has a given economic system is a fact about what the members of that society normally try to accomplish in producing and distributing goods; in short, it is an historical fact about the purposes which members of a given society normally have in mind in certain situations. Such historical facts have not as yet been explained by a general law, whether in economics or sociology. Marx's attempt so to explain the existence of capitalism was a brilliant but unmistakable failure. The only explanations we have of such facts, and we do not have many, are historical.

There is a lesson in this. In all societies there are certain departments of life in which most of their members normally seek certain ends and refuse to sanction certain means of attaining them. From such information it is often possible to deduce certain general truths about those societies; or even, as in the case of Gresham's Law, certain general truths about a whole class of similar societies. These general truths may also be discovered empirically, as Aristophanes discovered Gresham's Law to obtain in Athenian economy. But if the fact that such general truths hold good in a given society or class of societies is derivable from historical facts about the ways in which members of those societies normally think, and if those historical facts cannot themselves be explained as being based on a general law, then the social sciences which treat of such truths are not genuinely based on such a law. To the extent that what I have said of Gresham's Law is true of other economic and sociological laws, economics and sociology are not based on general laws, but fundamentally on historical facts. To what extent that is so, you must decide for yourselves.

From "Are the Social Sciences Really Historical?" by A. Donegan

1   What do the following terms mean in physical science? Fact—principle—generalization—law—theory.

2   Granted that good money does drive out bad (in a "pure" monetary economy), can you advance any hypothesis to explain this phenomenon? Would it be possible to test your hypothesis? If your experiments were successful, would you be any nearer to giving a scientific rather than an historical basis to Gresham's Law?

3   What do you consider to be the essential differences between the social and the physical sciences: areas of investigation; methods of inquiry; standpoint of the observer; validity of findings?

4   How does the writer dodge a very big issue in his final paragraph?

5   Are historical facts to the social scientist what measurements are to the physical scientist?

6   In 1955, the opponents of the introduction of commercial television in this country often "invoked Gresham's Law". What is the force of the analogy?

THE DOCKERS were given a commission of inquiry early in 1920, before which Ernest Bevin first made his name and which gave them greatly improved conditions. Bevin and Thomas, with all their differences, were outstanding union leaders of a new type. Though aggressively working class in character, they were no longer concerned merely to resist. Nor would they put off improvement till the distant dawn of socialism. They bargained with the employers as equals, displaying equal or greater skill, and never forgot that compromise was their ultimate aim, whether with a strike or preferably without.

The leaders of the miners had a different outlook. They fought class war, and the employers responded with zest. Birkenhead remarked after a meeting with the miners' representatives: "I should call them the stupidest men in England if I had not previously had to deal with the owners." The affairs of the coal industry dragged the whole nation into turmoil. In 1920 Great Britain was still booming, and the Labour movement was in high confidence. Labour candidates were steadily successful at by-elections. Henderson and other leaders found their way back to the House of Commons. Trade union membership reached a peak of over eight million. The Trades Union Congress replaced its ineffective parliamentary committee by a general council, which was presented, somewhat optimistically, as a "general staff" for industrial action. A national Council of Labour, representing the general council of the T.U.C., the national executive of the Labour party, and the parliamentary party, claimed to speak for "Labour" throughout the country.

Labour also found its voice in a more literal sense. A socialist daily newspaper appeared, the *Daily Herald*. It was edited by George Lansbury, revered leader of the emotional Left, and written for the most part by young middle-class intellectuals. Some of them, such as William Mellor and G. D. H. Cole, had already been socialists before the war. Others—Siegfried Sassoon, Osbert Sitwell, W. J. Turner—had become radicals as the result of their wartime experiences. All contributed a gay, self-confident contempt for the doings of the governing class. The *Daily Herald* had a hard struggle against the organs of the "capitalist" press. It never made ends meet in Lansbury's time, when it was still, of course, despite its socialist principles, a private venture. But it broke the old monopoly of established opinion and bore witness that the people of England were not all thinking as their rulers thought they should.

On the extreme Left, things were astir. The example of Soviet Russia was infectious. In July 1920 various revolutionary factions— principally the British Socialist party, with some support from the Socialist Labour Party of Glasgow, and shop stewards from Glasgow and Sheffield—set up the Communist Party of Great Britain in the inappropriate surroundings of the Cannon Street Hotel. The intention was to repeat Lenin's success, and to establish the dictatorship of the proletariat in Great Britain. The new party had few members, and these few did not understand what they had committed themselves to. It was eyed askance even by the I.L.P., the majority of whom refused after a long period of debate to put themselves under the orders of Moscow. The Labour Party, which had formerly taken in all and sundry, refused the affiliation which the Communists asked for on Lenin's instruction. The Labour Party had now a defined outlook of its own and was taking sides in the world-wide cleavage between democratic socialism and revolutionary Communism. Nevertheless the Communists had great influence in a watered-down way. Many, if not most, socialists shared their belief that capitalism was about to collapse and, like the Communists, blamed capitalism for "imperialist wars". Most socialists talked class war, though without any serious intention of using more violent weapons than the strike and the ballot box.

Plans for a general strike flourished in this atmosphere, and the idea received a shot in the arm from a demonstration of its practical effectiveness, a demonstration, moreover, of a directly political kind. In the summer of 1920 the threat of a general strike was used to stop a war. Though intervention against the Bolsheviks was virtually at an end, Poland and Russia were still at war. Early in 1920 the Poles set out to conquer the Ukraine, their old empire. Poland was disliked by moderate socialists, who sympathized with Germany; Soviet Russia was admired by the more extreme; all of them distrusted the British Government. On 10 May London dockers refused to load munitions for Poland on to the *Jolly George*. Labour men applauded, and the Government acquiesced in the ban while the Poles were winning. In July, however, the Poles were routed; the Red Army was in full march on Warsaw. The French were eager to intervene on the Polish side; Lloyd George, pushed on by Churchill and others, seemed ready to go along with them.

Labour acted in solid resistance. Councils of Action were set up in many towns. The National Council of Labour took control. Plans were made for an immediate general strike. Even the most cautious Labour leaders, such as Clynes and Thomas, were prepared to challenge "the whole Constitution of the country". On 10 August Bevin presented Labour's ultimatum. Lloyd George was delighted to turn the storm against his unruly colleagues. Labour, he said, was knocking at an open door so far as he was concerned; he even urged Bevin to act as negotiator between Russia and the British Government. The danger of war vanished overnight, partly no doubt because the Poles managed to save themselves without British assistance.

Nevertheless, it had been a glorious victory. Despite Lloyd George's subsequent denials, it is difficult to believe that there would have been no British aid to the Poles, if the threat of a general strike had not been made—and made with such unanimity. The door may have been open; a strong push was needed to send Lloyd George through it. Yet the victory had its misleading side. For once, that amorphous creature, public opinion, was on the side of unconstitutional action. Even the sanctity of parliamentary government has its limit. That limit was drawn by the war-weariness of the British people. "Hands off Soviet Russia" counted for something; "No More War" was irresistible.

From *English History 1914–1945* by A. J. P. Taylor

1   What are the main differences between democratic Socialism and revolutionary Communism? Which of these differences led the Labour Party to identify with the former?

2   What technical and organizational developments in the twentieth century have enabled "that amorphous creature, public opinion" to express itself more clearly, quickly, and effectively? Is it possible that these same, or parallel, developments might work in some ways to stifle, standardize, or enervate public opinion?

3   Consider the effectiveness of the disarmament movement in this country (do not confine your attention to CND). In what respects has it failed and in what respects has it succeeded? What conditions or methods might have helped it to translate its ideals into effective political action by the Government?

4   Does a national daily or Sunday newspaper form or reflect the opinions of its readers? Should organs of opinion depend for survival upon commercial success? Can diversity of opinion survive the mass media?

5   Consider some recent events that, by forcing issues, have accelerated the development of opinions, movements, or legislation.

6   Do the leaders of a democratically elected government try to enact the will of the people or are they more concerned to "educate" the will of the people to correspond with their own interpretation of the people's needs?

THE DIRECTOR opened a door. They were in a large bare room, very bright and sunny; for the whole of the southern wall was a single window. Half a dozen nurses, trousered and jacketed in the regulation white viscose-linen uniform, their hair aseptically hidden under white caps, were engaged in setting out bowls of roses in a long row across the floor. Big bowls, packed tight with blossom. Thousands of petals, ripe-blown and silkily smooth, like the cheeks of innumerable little cherubs, but of cherubs, in that bright light, not exclusively pink and Aryan, but also luminously Chinese, also Mexican, also apoplectic with too much blowing of celestial trumpets, also pale as death, pale with the posthumous whiteness of marble.

The nurses stiffened to attention as the D.H.C. came in.

"Set out the books," he said curtly.

In silence the nurses obeyed his command. Between the rose-bowls the books were duly set out—a row of nursery quartos opened invitingly each at some gaily coloured image of beast or fish or bird.

"Now bring in the children."

They hurried out of the room and returned in a minute or two, each pushing a kind of tall dumb-waiter laden, on all its four wire-netted shelves, with eight-month-old babies, all exactly alike (a Bokanovsky Group, it was evident) and all (since their caste was Delta) dressed in khaki.

"Put them down on the floor."

The infants were unloaded.

"Now turn them so that they can see the flowers and books."

Turned, the babies at once fell silent, then began to crawl towards those clusters of sleek colours, those shapes so gay and brilliant on the white pages. As they approached, the sun came out of a momentary eclipse behind a cloud. The roses flamed up as though with a sudden passion from within; a new and profound significance seemed to suffuse the shining pages of the books. From the ranks of the crawling babies came little squeals of excitement, gurgles and twitterings of pleasure.

The Director rubbed his hands. "Excellent!" he said. "It might almost have been done on purpose."

The swiftest crawlers were already at their goal. Small hands reached out uncertainly, touched, grasped, unpetalling the transfigured roses, crumpling the illuminated pages of the books. The Director waited until all were happily busy. Then, "Watch carefully," he said. And, lifting his hand, he gave the signal.

The Head Nurse, who was standing by a switchboard at the other end of the room, pressed down a little lever.

There was a violent explosion. Shriller and ever shriller, a siren shrieked. Alarm bells maddeningly sounded.

The children started, screamed; their faces were distorted with terror.

"And now," the Director shouted (for the noise was deafening), "now we proceed to rub in the lesson with a mild electric shock."

He waved his hand again, and the Head Nurse pressed a second lever. The screaming of the babies suddenly changed its tone. There was something desperate, almost insane, about the sharp spasmodic yelps to which they now gave utterance. Their little bodies twitched and stiffened; their limbs moved jerkily as if to the tug of unseen wires.

"We can electrify that whole strip of floor," bawled the Director in explanation. "But that's enough," he signalled to the nurse.

The explosion ceased, the bells stopped ringing, the shriek of the siren died down from tone to tone into silence. The stiffly twitching bodies relaxed, and what had become the sob and yelp of infant maniacs broadened out once more into a normal howl of ordinary terror.

"Offer them the flowers and the books again."

The nurses obeyed; but at the approach of the roses, at the mere sight of those gaily-coloured images of pussy and cock-a-doodle-doo and baa-baa black sheep, the infants shrank away in horror; the volume of their howling suddenly increased.

"Observe," said the Director triumphantly, "observe."

Books and loud noises, flowers and electric shocks—already in the infant mind these couples were compromisingly linked; and after two hundred repetitions of the same or a similar lesson would be wedded indissolubly. What man has joined, nature is powerless to put asunder.

"They'll grow up with what the psychologists used to call an "instinctive" hatred of books and flowers. Reflexes unalterably conditioned. They'll be safe from books and botany all their lives." The Director turned to his nurses. "Take them away again."

Still yelling, the khaki babies were loaded on to their dumb-waiters and wheeled out, leaving behind them the smell of sour milk and a most welcome silence.

One of the students held up his hand; and though he could see quite well why you couldn't have lower-caste people wasting the Community's time over books, and that there was always the risk of their reading something which might undesirably de-condition one of their reflexes, yet . . . well, he couldn't understand about the flowers. Why go to the trouble of making it psychologically impossible for Deltas to like flowers?

Patiently the D.H.C. explained. If the children were made to scream at the sight of a rose, that was on grounds of high economic policy. Not so very long ago (a century or thereabouts), Gammas, Deltas, even Epsilons, had been conditioned to like flowers—flowers in particular and wild nature in general. The idea was to make them want to be going out into the country at every available opportunity, and so compel them to consume transport.

"And didn't they consume transport?" asked the student.

"Quite a lot," the D.H.C. replied. "But nothing else."

From *Brave New World* by Aldous Huxley

1   What are the methods of classical and operant conditioning? What are the chief differences between the processes described as "brain-washing", "indoctrination", "training", and "education"? What use (if any) is being made of conditioning in education and training methods throughout the world?

2   What is the power—and the danger—of aphorisms such as "What man has joined, nature is powerless to put asunder"?

3   Are there any signs in the advanced industrial countries that the consumption of goods is being elevated to the status of a patriotic, even humanitarian duty? Is it fair to say that our patterns of consumption are already subjected to conditioning processes?

4   What can be done to prevent the Age of Specialization from becoming (via automation, mass markets, and mass media) the Age of Manipulation? Were the masses manipulated by the few in the

nineteenth century—in the fourteenth century? If so, what were the means of manipulation then?

5 Apart from the insult it offers to human dignity, what other changes lie in reliance upon manipulation?

Apart from the risk it imposes on human survival, what other dangers lie in insistence upon freedom of individual thought and action?

6 Do the prophecies contained in such books as *Brave New World*, *1984*, and *First and Last Men* serve any useful purpose?

BENJAMIN FELT a nose nuzzling at his shoulder. He looked round. It was Clover. Her old eyes looked dimmer than ever. Without saying anything, she tugged gently at his mane and led him round to the end of the big barn, where the Seven Commandments were written. For a minute or two they stood gazing at the tarred wall with its white lettering.

"My sight is failing," she said finally. "Even when I was young I could not have read what was written there. But it appears to me that that wall looks different. Are the Seven Commandments the same as they used to be, Benjamin?"

For once Benjamin consented to break his rule, and he read out to her what was written on the wall. There was nothing there now except a single Commandment. It ran:

ALL ANIMALS ARE EQUAL
BUT SOME ANIMALS ARE MORE
EQUAL THAN OTHERS

After that it did not seem strange when next day the pigs who were supervising the work of the farm all carried whips in their trotters. It did not seem strange to learn that the pigs had bought themselves a wireless set, were arranging to install a telephone, and had taken out subscriptions to *John Bull*, *Tit-Bits*, and the *Daily Mirror*. It did not seem strange when Napoleon was seen strolling in the farmhouse garden with a pipe in his mouth—no, not even when the pigs took Mr. Jones's clothes out of the wardrobes and put them on, Napoleon himself appearing in a black coat, ratcatcher breeches, and leather leggings, while his favourite sow appeared in the watered silk dress which Mrs. Jones had been used to wear on Sundays.

A week later, in the afternoon, a number of dog-carts drove up to the farm. A deputation of neighbouring farmers had been invited to make a tour of inspection. They were shown all over the farm, and expressed great admiration for everything they saw, especially the windmill. The animals were weeding the turnip field. They worked diligently, hardly raising their faces from the ground, and not knowing whether to be more frightened of the pigs or of the human visitors.

From *Animal Farm* by George Orwell

1 Having led the revolution against the farmer, Mr. Jones, the pigs have won power, abused power, and finally have been so corrupted by power that they assume the traditional trappings and luxuries of power and behave more ruthlessly than Jones himself had done. Must absolute power corrupt absolutely? How can the electors (who are equal) prevent those they choose to govern them from becoming more equal than others?

2 Is it true that the Establishment always successfully absorbs the anti-Establishment rebels in the community?

3 Consider some of the most powerful slogans of recent years. Why are they usually more effective than reasoned argument?

4 What advantages does the allegorical form offer to the didactic writer?

THE NINETEENTH century . . . was predominantly the century of transition for science. It was to change during those hundred years from an elegant ornament of society, practised by virtuosi, to an essential factor in the everyday production of goods and services. Science had in that time to fight its way into education and the professions. The process inevitably diverted much of its energy and the compromises it was forced to make necessarily weakened its capacities for advance.

The battle for scientific education and for the place of science in general education raged all through the century. Educational institutions are normally conservative and to find place for science in a curriculum already crammed with the relics of Renaissance humanism would have been difficult enough. But in the beginning of the nineteenth century another factor powerfully reinforced the resistance. Before 1788 science had been all the rage in the circles of the Enlightenment. Even if Oxford and Cambridge had been left "plunged in their dogmatic slumbers", the dissenting academies in England and the rejuvenated universities of Scotland had provided an education which balanced science and liberal sentiments. Similar movements took place in the enlightened despotisms from Spain to Russia. The

French Revolution changed all that. It now appeared that science, glorified by the Encyclopaedists and in which Voltaire had dabbled, not to mention the terrible Dr. Priestley, was a dangerous revolutionary doctrine, subversive to Church and King. Its spread, especially to the middle or even worse to the lower classes, needed to be sternly resisted. A similar reaction took place in France after the fall of Napoleon and throughout Europe under the Holy Alliance. Even in America, Franklin was forgotten and Priestley died in unhappy exile.

The reaction was not maintained—science came back with the reviving radicalism of the thirties, but the clergy and their landed and brewing supporters were well entrenched in the teaching profession and the battle went on for another sixty years at least, as witness the great evolution controversy. By the time it was over, both protagonists emerged very changed from their primitive state. Science, in particular, was very considerably denatured, with its conclusions watered down by agnosticism and its field of operation rigidly circumscribed to leave full play for a new spiritualized dogma, with less insistence on the literal interpretation of the first chapter of Genesis. Here, however, we are less concerned with this aspect than with the practical result that the facilities for learning any science at all remained very restricted throughout most of the century. What was taught in the older universities before their reform in 1877 was extremely formal and a young man who was interested in science had to pick it up as best he could. The new London colleges and the older Scottish ones gave more place to science but it was still largely theoretical. No practical science teaching was given in Britain, even in Cambridge, before 1845, and then it grew very slowly. . . .

Limited as were the opportunities for scientific training, those for research were even more so. France owed her scientific pre-eminence in the early nineteenth century to the great teaching centres of the Polytechnique and the Ecole Normale, but even there practical teaching was limited to specially favoured assistants of the professor. In Britain, research facilities hardly existed at all. . . .

The very comprehensive nature of scientific generalizations made their defenders sensitive to attack at any point. In the physical sciences it was the great tradition of Newton himself that was to be the greatest fetter on advance. Enshrined as it had become in the teaching of Cambridge and in the Council of the Royal Society, it dominated the physical outlook, determining at once which problems were deemed to be important and the proper mathematical way in which they should be studied. Newton's mechanical, mathematical universe was defended most fiercely on unessential points for fear of throwing nature back into chaos. . . .

It was characteristic that the new ideas could not penetrate from the centres of physical science in Cambridge or Paris but had to come from Germany, Scotland, or from Manchester—"where they ate their dinner in the middle of the day".

From *Science and Industry in the Nineteenth Century*
by J. D. Bernal

1 In this passage, Bernal examines those factors that restricted the opening of a great new channel of free human enquiry in the nineteenth century. Is science still restricted by those forces? Or are other antagonisms or restrictions on development now more powerful?

2 What forces could be identified in this country today as opposing or restraining the free development of artistic activity and experience?

3 What are the responsibilities of government towards the stimulation of research, invention, writing, and composition? How can it best foster the vigorous activity of the most fertile minds?

4 How can scientists and artists influence government to support their activities?

5 Is the generalization that "Educational institutions are normally conservative" justified? Is there any evidence that new areas and methods of study are being resisted by educational institutions today?

6 Bernal believes that in the nineteenth century the development of education in science owed more to the demands of technology than to anything else. Is this still true today?

7 Scientific method and accumulated knowledge help scientists to seek the right answers. How do they know which questions to ask?

WHAT THE Western world has stood for—and by that I mean the terms to which it has attributed sanctity—is "Liberalism" and "Democracy". The two terms are not identical or inseparable. The term "Liberalism" is the more obviously ambigious, and is now less in favour; but the term "Democracy" is at the height of its popularity. When a term has become so universally sanctified as "democracy" now is, I begin to wonder whether it means anything, in meaning too many things : it has arrived perhaps at the position of a Merovingian Emperor, and wherever it is invoked, one begins to look for the Major of the Palace. Some persons have gone so far as to affirm, as something self-evident, that democracy is the only regime compatible with Christianity. . . . If anybody ever attacked democracy, I might discover what the word meant. . . . Defenders of the totalitarian system can make out a plausible case for maintaining that what we have is not democracy, but financial oligarchy. . . .

That Liberalism may be a tendency towards something very different from itself, is a possibility in its nature. For it is something which tends to release energy rather than accumulate it, to relax, rather than to fortify. It is a movement not so much defined by its end, as by its starting point; away from, rather than towards, something definite. Our point of departure is more real to us than our destination; and the destination is likely to present a very different picture when arrived at, from the vaguer image formed in imagination. By destroying traditional social habits of the people, by dissolving their natural collective consciousness into individual constituents, by licensing the opinions of the most foolish, by substituting instruction for education, by encouraging cleverness rather than wisdom, the upstart rather than the qualified, by fostering a notion of getting on to which the alternative is a hopeless apathy, Liberalism can prepare the way for that which is its own negation: the artificial, mechanized or brutalized control which is a desperate remedy for its chaos.

It must be evident that I am speaking of Liberalism in a sense much wider than any which can be fully exemplified by the history of any political party, and equally in a wider sense than any in which it has been used in ecclesiastical controversy. True, the tendency of Liberalism can be more clearly illustrated in religious history than in politics, where principle is more diluted by necessity, where observation is more confused by detail and distracted by reforms each valid within its own limited reference. In religion, Liberalism may be characterized as a progressive discarding of elements in historical Christianity which appear superfluous or obsolete, confounded with practices and abuses which are legitimate objects of attack. But as its movement is controlled rather by its origin than by any goal, it loses force after a series of rejections, and with nothing to destroy is left with nothing to uphold and with nowhere to go. With religious Liberalism, however, I am no more specifically concerned than with political Liberalism: I am concerned with a state of mind which, in certain circumstances, can become universal and infect opponents as well as defenders. And I shall have expressed myself very ill if I give the impression that I think of Liberalism as something simply to be rejected and extirpated, as an evil for which there is a simple alternative. It is a necessary negative element; when I have said the worst of it, that worst comes only to this, that a negative element made to serve the purpose of a positive is objectionable. In the sense in which Liberalism is contrasted with Conservatism, both can be equally repellent: if the former can mean chaos, the latter can mean petrifaction. We are always faced with the question "What must be destroyed?" and with the question "What must be preserved?" and neither Liberalism nor Conservatism, which are not philosophies and may be merely habits, is enough to guide us. . . .

The attitudes and beliefs of Liberalism are destined to disappear, are already disappearing. They belong to an age of free exploitation which has passed; and our danger now is, that the term may come to signify for us only the disorder the fruits of which we inherit, and not the permanent value of the negative element. Out of Liberalism itself come philosophies which deny it. We do not proceed, from Liberalism to its apparent end of authoritarian democracy, at a uniform pace in every respect. . . . Furthermore, those who are the most convinced of the necessity of *étatisme* as a control of some activities of life, can be the loudest professors of libertarianism in others, and insist upon the preserves of "private life" in which each man may obey his own convictions or follow his own whim : while imperceptibly this domain of "private life" becomes smaller and smaller, and may eventually disappear altogether. . . .

If, then, Liberalism disappears from the philosophy of life of a people, what positive is left? We are left only with the term "democracy", a term which, for the present generation, still has a Liberal connotation of "freedom". But totalitarianism can retain the terms "freedom" and "democracy" and give them its own meaning : and its right to them is not so easily disproved as minds inflamed by passion suppose. We are in danger of finding ourselves with nothing to stand for except a dislike. . . . A dislike which, being a compost of newspaper sensations and prejudice, can have two results, at the same time, which appear at first incompatible. It may lead us to reject possible improvements, . . . and it may equally well lead us to be mere imitators *à rebours*, in making us adopt uncritically almost any attitude which a foreign nation rejects.

From *The Idea of a Christian Society* by T. S. Eliot

1 Try attacking the idea of "freedom" or "equality" or "progress".
Then, after the battle, consider whether you have come nearer to understanding what the word means.

2 Do you consider that there are any positive elements in Liberalism?
Or any negative elements in Conservatism?

3 "But as its movement is controlled rather by its origin than by any goal, it loses force after a series of rejections, and with nothing to destroy is left with nothing to uphold and with nowhere to go."
What do you think T. S. Eliot would have thought of TW3 and its

successors? In what sense has the negative element "permanent value"?

4   Can such terms as "freedom" and "democracy" honestly be given different meanings by different nations? Do different interpretations cause or exacerbate conflict? Or are they merely a sympton of it?

5   Can "dislike" create a country's policy?

6   "We are always faced with the question 'what must be destroyed?' and with the question 'what must be preserved?'"
Is this the heart of the dilemma that recurrs in different forms in the passages in this section?

Part Four

The Nature of Science

Since the Ancients (as we are told by Pappus) esteemed the science of mechanics of greatest importance in the investigation of natural things, and the moderns, rejecting substantial forms and occult qualities, have endeavoured to subject the phenomena of nature to the laws of mathematics, I have in this treatise cultivated mathematics as far as it relates to philosophy. The ancients considered mechanics in a twofold respect; as rational, which proceeds accurately by demonstration, and practical. To practical mechanics all the manual arts belong, from which mechanics took its name. But as artificers do not work with perfect accuracy, it comes to pass that mechanics is so distinguished from geometry that what is perfectly accurate is called geometrical; what is less so, is called mechanical. However, the errors are not in the art, but in the artificers. He that works with less accuracy is an imperfect mechanic; and if any could work with perfect accuracy, he would be the most perfect mechanic of all, for the description of right lines and circles, upon which geometry is founded, belongs to mechanics. Geometry does not teach us to draw lines, but requires them to be drawn, for it requires that the learner should first be taught to describe these accurately before he enters upon geometry, then it shows how by these operations problems may be solved.

To describe right lines and circles are problems, but not geometrical problems. The solution of these problems is required from mechanics, and by geometry the use of them, when so solved, is shown; and it is the glory of geometry that from these few principles, brought from without it, it is able to produce so many things. Therefore geometry is founded in mechanical practice, and is nothing but the part of universal mechanics which accurately proposes and demonstrates the art of measuring. But since the manual arts are chiefly employed in the moving of bodies, it happens that geometry is commonly referred to their magnitude, and mechanics to their motion. In this case rational mechanics will be the science of motions resulting from any forces whatsoever, and of the forces required to produce any motions accurately proposed and demonstrated. This part of mechanics, as far as it extended to the five powers which relate to manual parts, was cultivated by the ancients, who considered gravity (it not being a manual power) no otherwise than in moving weights by those powers. But I consider philosophy rather than arts and write not concerning manual but natural powers, and consider chiefly those things which relate to gravity, levity, elastic force, the resistance of fluids, and the forces, whether attractive or impulsive; and therefore I offer this work as the mathematical principles of philosophy, for the whole burden of philosophy seems to consist in this — from the phenomena of motions to investigate the forces of nature, and then from these forces to demonstrate the other phenomena; and to this end the general propositions in the first and second Books are directed. In the third Book I give an example of this in the explication of the system of the World; for by the propositions mathematically demonstrated in the former books, in the third I derive from the celestial phenomena the forces of gravity with which bodies tend to the sun and the several planets. Then from these forces, by other propositions which are also mathematical, I deduce the motions of the planets, the comets, the moon, and the sea. I wish we could derive the rest of the phenomena of Nature by the same kind of reasoning from mechanical principles, for I am induced by many reasons to suspect that they may all depend upon certain forces by which the particles of the bodies, by some cause hitherto unknown, are either mutually impelled towards one another, and cohere in regular figures, or are repelled and recede from one another. These forces being unknown, philosophers have hitherto attempted the search of Nature in vain; but I hope the principles here laid down will afford some light either to this or some truer method of philosophy.

In the publication of this work the most acute and universally learned Mr. Edmond Halley not only assisted me in correcting the errors of the press and preparing the geometrical figures, but it was through his solicitations that it came to be published; for when he had obtained of me my demonstrations of the figure of the celestial orbits, he continually pressed me to communicate the same to the Royal Society, who afterwards, by their kind encouragement and entreaties, engaged me to think of publishing them. But after I had begun to consider the inequalities of the lunar motions, and had entered upon some other things unrelating to the laws and measures of gravity and other forces; and the figures that would be described by bodies attracted according to given laws; and the motion of several bodies moving among themselves; the motion of bodies in resisting mediums; the forces, densities and motions, of mediums; the orbits of the comets, and such like, I deferred that publication till I had made a search into these matters, and could put forth the whole together. What relates to the lunar motions (being imperfect), I have put all together in the corollaries of Prop. LXVI, to avoid being obliged to propose and distinctly demonstrate the several things there contained in a method more prolix than the subject deserved and interrupt the series of the other propositions. Some things, found out after the rest, I chose to insert in places less suitable, rather than change the number of the propositions and the citations. I heartily beg that what I have done may be read with forbearance; and that my labours in a subject so difficult may be examined, not so much with the view to censure, as to remedy their defects.

From *The Mathematical Principles of Natural Philosophy*
by Isaac Newton

1 Of what value are the distinctions Newton makes between geometry and mechanics?

2 Are there any correspondences between these distinctions and the distinctions currently made between the pure and applied sciences? In what respects are these latter distinctions useful, and in what respects harmful?

3 What constitutes a "professional scientific attitude"? Does Newton appear to live up to today's ideal?

4 What part should speculation, suspicion, and emotion play in scientific inquiry?

I STAND at the window of a railway carriage which is travelling uniformly, and drop a stone on the embankment, without throwing it. Then disregarding the influence of the air resistance, I see the stone descend in a straight line. A pedestrian who observes the misdeed from the footpath notices that the stone falls to earth in a parabolic curve. I now ask: Do the "positions" traversed by the stone lie "in reality" on a straight line or on a parabola? Moreover, what is meant here by motion "in space"? . . . In the first place, we entirely shun the vague word "space", of which, we must honestly acknowledge, we cannot form the slightest conception, and we replace it by "motion relative to a practically rigid body of reference". If instead of "body of reference" we insert "system of co-ordinates" which is a useful idea for mathematical description, we are in a position to say: The stone traverses a straight line relative to a system of co-ordinates rigidly attached to the carriage, but relative to a system of co-ordinates rigidly attached to the ground (embankment) it describes a parabola. With the aid of this example it is clearly seen that there is no such thing as an independently existing trajectory (literally, "path-curve"), but only a trajectory relative to a particular body of reference.

In order to have a complete description of the motion we must specify how the body alters its position with time; i.e., for every point on the trajectory it must be stated at what time the body is situated there. These data must be supplemented by such a definition of time that, in virtue of this definition, these time values can be regarded essentially as magnitudes (results of measurements) capable of observation. If we take our stand on the ground of classical mechanics, we can satisfy this requirement for our illustration in the following manner. We imagine two clocks of identical construction; the man at the railway-carriage window is holding one of them, and the man on the footpath the other. Each of the observers determines the position on his own reference body occupied by the stone at each tick of the clock he is holding in his hand. In this connection we have not taken account of the inaccuracy involved by the finiteness of the velocity of propagation of light. With this and with a second difficulty prevailing here we shall have to deal in detail later.

Now in virtue of its motion in an orbit round the sun, our earth is comparable with a railway carriage travelling with a velocity of about 30 kilometres per second. If the principle of relativity were not valid we should therefore expect that the direction of motion of the earth at any moment would enter into the laws of nature, and also that physical systems in their behaviour would be dependent on the orientation in space with respect to the earth.

However, the most careful observations have never revealed such anisotropic properties in terrestrial physical space, i.e., a physical non-equivalence of different directions. This is very powerful argument in favour of the principle of relativity.

There is hardly a simpler law in physics than that according to which light is propagated in empty space. Every child at school knows, or believes he knows, that this propagation takes place in straight lines with a velocity $c = 300,000$ km/sec. At all events we know with great exactness that this velocity is the same for all colours, because if this were not the case, the minimum of emission would not be observed simultaneously for different colours during the eclipse of a fixed star by its dark neighbour. By means of similar considerations based on observations of double stars, the Dutch astronomer De Sitter was also able to show that the velocity of propagation of light cannot depend on the velocity of motion of the body emitting the light. The assumption that this velocity of propagation is dependent on the direction "in space" is in itself improbable.

Lightning has struck the rails on our railway embankment at two places A and B far distant from each other. I make the additional assertion that these two lightning flashes occurred simultaneously. If I ask you whether there is sense in this statement, you will answer my question with a decided "Yes". But if I now approach you with the request to explain to me the sense of the statement more precisely, you find after some consideration that the answer to this question is not so easy as it appears at first sight.

Are two events (e.g., the two strokes of lightning A and B) which are simultaneous with reference to the railway embankment also simultaneous relatively to the train? We shall show directly that the answer must be in the negative.

When we say that the lightning strokes A and B are simultaneous with respect to the embankment, we mean : the rays of light emitted at the places A and B, where the lightning occurs, meet each other at the mid-point M of the length A-B of the embankment. But the events A and B also correspond to positions A and B on the train. Let M' be the mid-point of the distance A-B on the travelling train. Just when the flashes of lightning occur, this point M' naturally coincides with the point M, but it moves towards the right (in a diagram) with the velocity of the train. If an observer sitting in the position M' in the train did not possess this velocity, then he would remain permanently at M, and the light rays emitted by the flashes of lightning A and B would reach him simultaneously, i.e., they would meet just where he is situated. Now in reality (considered with reference to the railway embankment) he is hastening towards the beam of light coming from B, whilst he is riding on ahead of the beam of light coming from A. Hence the observer will see the beam of light emitted from B earlier than he will see that emitted from A. Observers who take the railway train as their reference body must therefore come to the conclusion that the lightning flash B took place earlier than the lightning flash A. We thus arrive at the important result:

Events which are simultaneous with reference to the embankment are not simultaneous with respect to the train, and vice versa (relativity of simultaneity).

From *Relativity, the Special and General Theory*
by A. Einstein

1   Is Einstein successful in conveying understanding of a difficult concept? What means does he employ?

2   In scientific writing, what are the advantages and limitations of exemplification?

3   Many of the greatest discoveries, if adequately explained, prompt men to ask, "Well, why didn't somebody think of that before?" Is it possible to generalize about psychological and physical barriers to inquiry?

4   Has the principle of relativity had any effect on methods in the natural and social sciences?

IF A well were sunk at our feet in the midst of the city of Norwich, the diggers would very soon find themselves at work in that white substance almost too soft to be called rock, with which we are all familiar as "chalk".

Not only here but over the whole county of Norfolk, the well sinker might carry his shaft down many hundred feet without coming to the end of the chalk; and, on the seacoast, where the waves have pared away the face of the land which breasts them, the scarped faces of the high cliffs are often wholly formed of the same material. . . .

What is this widespread component of the surface of the earth and whence did it come?

You may think this no very hopeful inquiry. You may not unnaturally suppose that the attempt to solve such problems as these can lead to no result, save that of entangling the inquirer in vague speculations, incapable of refutation and of verification. If such were really the case, I should have selected some other subject than a "piece of chalk" for my discourse. But in truth, after much deliberation, I have been unable to think of any topic which would so well enable me to lead you to see how solid is the foundation upon which some of the most startling conclusions of physical science rest.

A great chapter of the history of the world is written in the chalk. Few passages in the history of man can be supported by such an overwhelming mass of direct and indirect evidence as that which testifies to the truth of the fragment of the history of the globe, which I hope to enable you to read with your own eyes tonight. Let me add that few chapters of human history have a more profound significance for ourselves. I weigh my words well when I assert that the man who should know the true history of the bit of chalk which every carpenter carries about in his breeches pocket, though ignorant of all other history, is likely, if he will think his knowledge out to its ultimate results, to have a truer, and therefore a better, conception of this wonderful universe and of man's relation to it than the most learned student who is deep-read in the records of humanity and ignorant of those of nature. . .

To the unassisted eye chalk looks simply like a very loose and open kind of stone. But it presents a totally different appearance when placed under the microscope. The general mass of it is made up of very minute granules; but imbedded in this matrix are innumerable bodies, some smaller and some larger, but on a rough average not more than a hundredth of an inch in diameter, having a well-defined shape and structure. A cubic inch of some specimens of chalk may contain hundreds of thousands of these bodies, compacted together with incalculable millions of the granules. . . . Each of the rounded bodies may be proved to be a beautifully constructed calcareous fabric, made up of a number of chambers communicating freely with one another. The chambered bodies are of various forms. One of the commonest is something like a badly grown raspberry, being formed of a number of nearly globular chambers of different sizes congregated together. It is called globigerina, and some specimens of chalk consist of little else than globigerinae and granules. Let us fix our attention upon the globigerina. It is the spoor of the game we are tracking. If we can learn what it is and what are the conditions of its existence, we shall see our way to the origin and past history of the chalk. . . .

It so happens that calcareous skeletons, exactly similar to the globigerinae of the chalk, are being formed at the present moment by minute living creatures which flourish in multitudes, literally more numerous than the sands of the sea-shore, over a large extent of that part of the earth's surface which is covered by the ocean. . . .

In 1853, Lieutenant Brooke obtained mud from the bottom of the North Atlantic, between Newfoundland and the Azores, at a depth of more than ten thousand feet, or two miles, by the help of sounding apparatus. The specimens were sent for examination to Ehrenberg, of Berlin, and to Bailey, of West Point, and those able microscopists found that this deep-sea mud was almost entirely composed of the skeletons of living organisms—the great proportion of these being just like the globigerinae already known to occur in the chalk. . . .

However, the important points for us are that the living globigerinae are exclusively marine animals, the skeletons of which abound at the bottom of deep seas; and that there is not a shadow of reason for believing that the habits of the globigerinae of the chalk differed from those of the existing species. But if this be true, there is no escaping the conclusion that the chalk itself is the dried mud of an ancient deep sea. . . .

Thus evidence which cannot be rebutted, and which need not be strengthened, though if time permitted I might indefinitely increase its quantity, compels you to believe that the earth, from the time of the chalk to the present day, has been the theatre of a series of changes as vast in their amount as they were slow in their progress. The area on which we stand has been first sea and then land, for at least four alternations; and has remained in each of these conditions for a period of great length. . . .

But, great as is the magnitude of these physical changes of the world, they have been accompanied by a no less striking series of modifications in its living inhabitants. All the great classes of animals, beasts of the field, fowls of the air, creeping things, and things which dwell in the waters flourished upon the globe long ages before the chalk was deposited. Very few, however, if any, of these ancient forms of animal life were identical with those which now live. Certainly not one of the higher animals was of the same species as any of those now in existence. The beasts of the field, in the days before the chalk, were not our beasts of the field, nor the fowls of the air such as those which the eye of man has seen flying unless his antiquity dates infinitely further back than we at present surmise.

From "On a Piece of Chalk" by T. H. Huxley

1   Magnification has proved to be one of the most important tools of scientific enquiry. Dispute the relative merits of the other main tools of science.

2   Is Huxley's claim for the better understanding of the man who knows all about the carpenter's piece of chalk really justified?

3   Those who rhapsodize about "the romance of science" often delve into geological studies for their examples. Is geology a pure science? Or is it rather a classification-cum-narrative study, like geography?

4   What do you expect of a good lecture? What purposes had Huxley in mind when he delivered this lecture? How did he try to achieve these purposes?

5   Man has discovered through science that the earth is not the centre of the universe, nor himself a discrete creation. Has his egocentricity been tempered or has he rather sought new patterns of self-absorption?

6   Consider some other common substance or phenomenon that could be used to kindle the imagination and understanding.

IT WOULD be hard to imagine a more fundamental or more sweeping discovery than one elucidating, at a deeper level than had hitherto been imagined, the manner in which the information governing all the qualities of inheritance may be recorded and stored in the chromosomes of plants and animals and men—stored with such extraordinary effectiveness and such enduring stability that there are organisms living today whose hereditary characteristics have been maintained more durably than the very rocks within whose strata the fossils of their remote ancestors are preserved. Yet in terms of magnitude the human and the material resources committed to that search, by comparison with the preceding illustrations, have been positively minuscule.

In 1953 Linus Pauling and Robert Brainard Corey at the California Institute of Technology suggested that the molecular structure of the unit of heredity, the "molecule" of deoxyribonucleic acid, might consist of chains of polynucleotides intertwined in the form of a helix, with four characteristic bases, the purines adenine and guanine and the pyrimidines thymine and cytosine, attached to them and projecting outwards, while phosphate groups were oriented to the centre. There were features of this model which conflicted with experimental evidence, notably that it was hard to reconcile the fact that DNA is an acid with the existence of bases lying, as it were, on the outside of the molecule. But the model involved one very great idea which, though it was not widely credible in terms of that particular construction, yet was to prove fundamental to all further thinking on the matter. It was the idea that the biological specificity of the unit of DNA, on which its power of determining inheritance must rest, must inhere in the sequence of occurrence of these bases along the molecular chain and the suggestion that the periodic distance at which these bases occur might be of the right order to permit them to order the sequence of amino acids in the construction of a protein. This was a most important foundation upon which to rear what would prove a truly extraordinary arch of reasoning. But for long even the idea that the nucleic acid structure could be locally specific was resisted. Until that idea had been widely accepted, its more detailed consequence could hardly gain effective credence. Both these developments were made possible by a second great idea, which might be likened to a keystone of the arch.

This critical idea was provided by J. D. Watson when, in a flash of insight reminiscent of Kekulé's vision of the structure of the benzene molecule that came to him in a London bus almost a hundred years ago, he imagined the consequences of, in effect, turning the model inside out, pointing the bases inwards, and pairing the purine molecules with the smaller pyrimidines. Highly significant correspondences with nature were achieved by this remarkable insight. The first and fundamental rule of the composition of deoxyribonucleic acid, namely that it incorporates purines and pyrimidines in equal ratio, was given a rational basis. And the contradiction between the acidic nature of DNA and its presumed outwardly pointing bases, which had plagued the model of Pauling and Corey, was resolved. But there were impressive difficulties to be met also. The idea that the bases were outward-pointing had not resulted simply from neglecting the alternative that they might point inwards. That possibility, indeed, had been carefully examined in formulating the earlier model. But it had been concluded that such a structure was not possible. For the new model to be convincing, the physical possibility of such an arrangement had to be demonstrated, and the details of the linkages between the purines and pyrimidines had to be worked out—formidable tasks requiring concepts and techniques familiar to those dealing with the structure of crystals.

And so it was that, also in 1953, Watson and F. H. C. Crick, working in the Molecular Biology Unit of the British Medical Research Council adjacent to the Cavendish Laboratory at Cambridge, announced their brilliant hypothesis of the structure of the unit of heredity, of the "molecule" of deoxyribonucleic acid, as a pair of "ribbons" wound in the form of a double helix around a common axis and linked by the four bases, the purines adenine and guanine and the pyrimidines thymine and cytosine, paired in a highly specific fashion. The model of Pauling and Corey had suggested that the bases could not be packed in the centre of the molecule. The new model proved that indeed they could, and from that demonstration came perhaps the most significant idea in the whole chain—the concept of base pairing itself, and with it the associated and important notion that a maximum of four kinds of base pairs could be involved. The beauty and credibility of the model gave firmness and emphasis to the earlier idea that the biological specificity of the unit of heredity must derive in large measure from the ordering of the pairs of bases along the chain of the deoxyribonucleic acid.

From The Report of the President
on the Sixtieth Anniversary of the Carnegie Institution
for 1961–1962 by Caryl P. Haskins

1 Why are models so important to the scientist?

2 The social scientists also use models (e.g. of class structure). What precautions can they take to minimize the dangers that may be inherent in such practices?

3 The idea of turning the model inside out and pointing the bases inwards "had been carefully examined in formulating the earlier model." In what respect, then, was J. D. Watson's idea a "flash of insight"? In what ways, and at what times, can a scientist really use his imagination?

4 What other discoveries might lay claim to being "more fundamental or more sweeping" than the discovery of the structure of the DNA molecule?

5 In *Brave New World* Huxley envisaged complete State control of the kinds of babies produced—so many alphas, so many betas, gammas, deltas, and so on. In the light of past experience of the perverted uses to which science can be put, should governments seriously consider exercising strict control over biological investigations? Or should the scientists themselves hold back?

FOR MORE than two thousand years the attraction of light bodies by amber was the sum of human knowledge regarding electricity, and for more than two thousand years fermentation was effected without any knowledge of its cause. In science one discovery grows out of another, and cannot appear without its proper antecedent. Thus, before fermentation could be understood, the microscope had to be invented, and brought to a considerable degree of perfection. Note the growth of knowledge. Leeuwenhoek, in 1680, found yeast to be a mass of floating globules, but he had no notion that the globules were alive. This was proved in 1835 by Cagniard de la Tour and Schwann. Then came the question as to the origin of such microscopic organisms, and in this connection the memoir of Pasteur, published in the *Annales de Chimie* for 1862, is the inauguration of a new epoch. . . . On that investigation all Pasteur's subsequent labours were based. Ravages had over and over again occurred among French wines. There was no guarantee that they would not become acid or bitter, particularly when exported. The commerce in wines was thus restricted, and disastrous losses were often inflicted on the wine-grower. Every one of these diseases was traced to the life of an organism. Pasteur ascertained the temperature which killed these ferments of disease, proving it to be so low as to be perfectly harmless to the wine. By the simple expedient of heating the wine to a temperature of fifty degrees centigrade, he rendered it inalterable, and thus saved his country the loss of millions. . . .

There are other reflections connected with this subject which, even were they now passed over without remark, would sooner or later occur to every thoughtful mind in this assembly. I have spoken of the floating dust of the air, of the means of rendering it visible, and of the perfect immunity from putrefaction which accompanies the contact of germless infusions and moteless air. Consider the woes which these wafted particles, during historic and pre-historic ages, have inflicted on mankind; consider the loss of life in hospitals from putrefying wounds; consider the loss in places where there are plenty of wounds, but no hospitals, and in the ages before hospitals were anywhere founded; consider the slaughter which has hitherto followed that of the battlefield, when those bacterial destroyers are let loose, often producing a mortality far greater than that of the battle itself; add to this the other conception that in times of epidemic disease the self-same floating matter has mingled with it the special germs which produce the epidemic, being thus enabled to sow pestilence and death over nations and continents—consider all this, and you will come with me to the conclusion that all the havoc of war, ten times multiplied, would be evanescent if compared with the ravages due to atmospheric dust.

This preventible destruction is going on today, and it has been permitted to go on for ages, without a whisper of information regarding its cause being vouchsafed to the suffering sentient world. We have been scourged by invisible thongs, attacked from inpenetrable ambuscades, and it is only today that the light of science is being let in upon the murderous dominion of our foes. Facts like these excite in me the thought that the rule and governance of this universe are different from what we in our youth supposed them to be—that the inscrutable Power, at once terrible and beneficent, in whom we live and move and have our beginning and our end, is to be propitiated by means different from those usually resorted to. The first requisite towards such propitiation is knowledge; the second is action, shaped and illuminated by that knowledge. Of knowledge we already see the dawn, which will open out by-and-by to perfect day; while the action which is to follow has its unfailing source and stimulus in the moral and emotional nature of man—in his desire for personal well-being, in his sense of duty, in his compassionate sympathy with the sufferings of his fellow-men. "How often," says Dr. William Budd in his celebrated work on Typhoid Fever—"How often have I seen in past days, in the single narrow chamber of the day-labourer's cottage the father in the coffin, the mother in the sick-bed in muttering delirium, and nothing to relieve the desolation of the children but the devotion of some poor neighbour, who in too many cases paid the penalty of her kindness in becoming herself the victim of the same disorder!" From the vantage ground already won I look forward with confident hope to the triumph of medical art over scenes of misery like that here described. The cause of the calamity being once clearly revealed, not only to the physician. but to the public, whose intelligent co-operation is absolutely essential to success, the final victory of humanity is only a question of time. We have already a foretaste of that victory in the triumphs of surgery as practised at your doors.

From "Fermentation and its Bearing on Surgery and Medicine"
by John Tyndall

1   Consider the various stimuli of scientific discovery mentioned in this extract: the accumulation of scientific knowledge; the invention of new or better scientific tools; economic or technological demand. What other stimuli are there?

2   Why have the victories of science received less recognition than the victories of war?

3   Does science need good propagandists? How might they set about their task?

4   The pace of scientific discovery accelerates every day. Now that we have reached the stage where scientific knowledge doubles every ten years, in what ways are the conditions affecting scientific discovery different from those in previous centuries?

5   Increasingly, scientific activity demands considerable resources, Should these be at the direction of government, industrial corporations,

or universities? Should government take the responsibility of establishing the order of priorities for scientific research?

6 Do you think it probable that the findings of social scientists will be as beneficial to mankind as the discoveries of such men as Pasteur?

ALTHOUGH THOROUGHLY investigated in the guinea pig, experimental scurvy has not been studied in the human adult. Indeed, until recently there seemed little to warrant such a study. The numerous and widespread clinical reports of scorbutus dating back to Hippocrates have drawn a detailed and comprehensive picture of the disease. With the discovery of other vitamins and the isolation of vitamin C, however, the question arises as to what roles such factors as multiple avitaminosis and infection may have played in the syndrome of scurvy and its complications. Obviously the vast majority of cases comprising the literature of this subject involve not only vitamin C deficiency but also multiple subclinical avitaminosis as well; and in many cases infection is an additional complicating factor. Moreover, with the recent development of methods for the determination of ascorbic acid* in the blood and urine, the necessity has arisen for correlating various blood and urine levels with degrees of pure vitamin C deficiency uncomplicated by other factors.

How long, for example, does it take for an adult on a diet entirely deficient in only vitamin C to become scorbutic? The crews of seventeenth-century and eighteenth-century sailing-vessels, having rations undoubtedly poor in many vitamins, frequently developed signs of scurvy after sixty to one hundred and twenty days at sea. Stark, in 1769, produced scorbutus and also some symptoms of vitamin B deficiency in himself by subsisting on a diet of bread and water for ten weeks, an effort which later resulted in his death.

In other communications we have presented partial data concerning an adult male on a diet totally deficient in vitamin C, but supplemented by all the other known vitamins. We now present the completed experiment in detail, representing six months of total vitamin C deficiency. To our knowledge, no controlled vitamin C deficiency has previously been carried longer than twelve days, although Van Eekelen remained on an uncontrolled vitamin C deficient diet for eighty-four days.

* Ascorbic acid is the scientific name for vitamin C.

EXPERIMENTAL DATA

J. H. C., a male adult weighing one hundred and fifty-eight pounds, with a negative history, physical examination and laboratory findings, placed himself on a diet containing no milk and no fruit or vegetables of any kind. . . .

During the first four months of the deficient diet all physical findings were negative. There was a slight fall in weight and basal metabolic rate and a feeling of easy fatiguability and slight weakness.

After one hundred and thirty-four days had elapsed, small perifollicular hyperkeratotic papules began to develop over the buttocks and the posterior aspects of the calves. There was noticeable fragmentation of hairs. These lesions, which progressed in severity during the ensuing three weeks, resembled a mild form of the lesion described as typical of vitamin A deficiency. Each papule contained an ingrown hair, which could be seen if the hyperkeratotic plug was picked or scraped off, leaving a small, slightly bleeding crater. Associated with these papules was a marked dryness of the skin, particularly over the exterior surfaces, and the backs of the hands became markedly roughened, the pores standing out in exaggerated fashion. The similarity between the lesions of vitamin A deficiency and those of vitamin C deficiency has been previously pointed out. . . .

After one hundred and sixty-one days of the diet, there appeared for the first time small perifollicular haemorrhages or petechiae over the lower legs. These lesions did not fade on pressure and were not elevated. They seemed to occur in greatest numbers after the subject had been standing for some time (five hours), appearing for the first time, in fact, following a long period of operating. First seen over the inner and extensor aspects of the lower legs, the petechiae crept upward as the experiment progressed, until at the end of six months they were abundant over the lower thighs, where they seemed to take the place of the hyperkeratotic lesions already described.

Wound Healing

At the end of three months, a sizable wound was made in the right mid-back of the subject. Ten days later biopsy of this wound showed good healing. At the end of one hundred and eighty-two days, a similar wound was made in the left mid-back.

The skin sutures were removed on the sixth post-operative day, at which time the wound seemed to be progressing normally.

On the tenth post-operative day, under Pentothal anaesthesia, a biopsy was made of the wound through an incision transverse to it and again extending down to the sacrospinalis muscle. Beneath the skin, which appeared well healed, there was no healing of the wound, which was filled with unorganized blood clot. This was in marked contra-distinction to the findings at three months, when there was perfect wound healing. So little healing had occurred that it was necessary to insert a small rubber drain, and the wound was brought together only with silk sutures through skin and subcutaneous tissue. . . .

Weight Loss

There was a gradual and continual weight loss for the first five and a half months of the experimental period, reaching a maximum of 27 pounds at the end of this time. This drop in weight can be criticized as adding an additional unknown factor to the experiment. We believe it difficult, however, for anyone to remain on a diet absolutely free of vitamin C over a long period without losing weight, since in order to avoid traces of the vitamin the diet must be restricted essentially to eggs, cheese, bread, butter, and sucrose.

Fatigue

From the beginning of the third month of the diet there developed a feeling of fatigue which became progressively more marked. . . .

At the end of the six months a fatigue test was carried out at the Fatigue Laboratory of Harvard University. In order to determine the extent to which the capacity for work was reduced and to learn something about the mechanisms involved, the subject performed two grades of work on a motor-driven treadmill (walking and running). After ten days, during which the subject received vitamin C intravenously but remained on the deficiency diet, the experiment was repeated. A control test was made seven weeks after the normal diet had been resumed. The data of Robinson covering the same age-group were used for comparison.

During a period of moderate work—a walk for four and a half minutes on a grade of 8·6 per cent at a rate of 3·5 miles per hour—both before and ten days after the beginning of vitamin C therapy, the subject's heart rate was nearly maximal, being about 40 beats per minute higher than on any of the men studied by Robinson. In the control test seven weeks later the heart rate after the same work was within normal limits. . . .

During a harder grade of work—a run at a rate of 7 miles an hour to exhaustion—the subject's performances while in the scorbutic state and directly after the vitamin C therapy showed considerable differences. In the state of complete vitamin C deficiency he was able to run for only 16 seconds, whereas following ascorbic acid therapy he ran for 66 seconds. . . .

The performance of the subject while in the scorbutic state placed him in the same category as the Group X of Robinson, consisting of men in the eighth decade of life, for whom the five-minute walk was maximal work.

From "Wound Healing and Vitamin C"
by J. H. Crandon, C. C. Lind, and D. B. Dill

1 What ethical questions arise in the planning and carrying out of experiments on: (i) living human beings, (ii) living animals?
Should political and social experiments be submitted to the same scrutiny?

2 What is the best way to teach a student scientist how to observe accurately and with patience?

3 How might the scientific correspondent of a quality newspaper have reported this experiment and drawn attention to its significance?

4 What was the compulsion that made J.H.C. submit to having wounds inflicted on his back and to the long rigours of this experiment that reduced his condition to that of a sick man of 70?

MY MAIN object in writing this article is to encourage people to think ahead into time when there will be plenty of time for doing, not what must be done for earning a living, but what one is interested in. Even economists are beginning to concede that the human capacity to consume more and more worldly goods is not infinitely extensible, even when stimulated by all kinds of artful devices and propaganda. In the advanced countries signs of satiation begin to be obvious. In the backward countries too, despite the fashionable Malthusian gloom, a good living could be obtained in the foreseeable future. People already talk and write *ad nauseam* about "the problem of leisure". It is indeed a problem in a society which has little respect for education, regarding it as a machine for the mass production and technical training of functionaries. But when free access to a liberal education has been provided for all I doubt if people will find it difficult to develop all kinds of constructive and absorbing interests that will cause their only regret to be the speed at which a human lifetime runs itself out. And one direction which such interests will take will increasingly be devotion to natural science.

Even at present, with all the irritating and unpleasant features outlined above, scientific research provides a satisfying life's work for many people, and those who work at narrow problems in applied science are often no less happy than those dealing with the most abstract and academic fields. As in other fields of creative endeavour, different temperaments are suited by different kinds of scientific work. Some people delight in theorizing, often in a speculative manner, on the basis of a few facts or principles, and from time to time come forward with some novel idea which can be tested by experiment. Others persevere in making systematic experiments or observations, hoping from these to arrive at some unifying principle. Of this approach, Charles Darwin's formulation of the theory of evolution is the outstanding example. Others occupy themselves mainly with improving methods of experiment or observation, thereby often lighting upon entirely new and unsuspected phenomena. Yet others keep a critical and encyclopaedic eye on a whole wide field, stepping in occasionally with an experiment that clears up an apparent inconsistency, or, better, opens up an entirely new approach to a subject. The final stage in the elucidation of the chemical structure of the sterols is a good example of this.

In all these kinds of research, on wide or narrow topics, there come moments of exaltation. Yet sometimes the grander generalizations about nature emerge only as a result of the sheer hard work of many people, often undertaken with a wide variety of motives. Thus it has only gradually and recently become apparent that proteins, which bulk large in all living organisms, are constructed throughout living nature from the same twenty amino acids. This, one of the most important facts in biology, was not "discovered" by any individual or group, and all the hundreds who have had a hand in the work, even in the negative activity of shortening the list, can feel pride. On other occasions important discoveries are prevented by barriers in the mind, which nobody manages to step over. Radioactive carbon has existed on the Earth throughout geological time. Yet not long ago nuclear physicists told us that no long-lived radioactive carbon could be expected. It was not till after it had, unpredictedly, been manufactured by bombardment that anybody looked for it in nature. As soon as it was found, there resulted a completely new method of dating in archaeology and quaternary geology, applicable to specimens many thousands of years old.

To contemplate the grander and unexpected advances of natural knowledge does good to the souls of all engaged in scientific work, and of many outside it. But such moments of exaltation are usually interspersed with long spells of hard and often rather dull work—describing, filling in gaps, and so forth, which do good to the soul in the more colloquial sense. Evolution has endowed us with a satisfaction from doing and completing plain hard work, for which no substitute has yet been discovered.

Moreover, many of us like at times to detach ourselves from the grand generalizations and to get pleasure from simple contemplation of the diversity of nature. We need no longer confine ourselves to the traditional branches of natural history, but can immerse ourselves in the chemistry of plant pigments or perfume, the antigenic specificity of bacteria, the antibiotic activities of fungi, and so on. . . .

What is needed demands a breaking down of many barriers, prejudices, and privileges. Children could attend schools freely for as long as they felt they were getting advantage from being at school. Research workers could devote a proportion of their time to teaching in school or university (even more necessary at the present time than it will be later). Universities could modify their regulations so that students could interrupt their courses, take part-time courses, and also take different courses at different universities. Students could spend time on farms, in factories, in hospitals, or as laboratory assistants before or during their periods of study. Far better opportunities could be provided for part-time study up to and beyond university standards. The same is true of facilities for part-time research; more and more of our expensive research equipment stands idle during the 128 hours of each week that do not lie between 9 a.m. and 5 p.m. from Mondays to Fridays. . . .

In essence, this natural historian's plea is for the restoration of something which has tended to become lost as civilization has become more complicated—that is, a view of humanity in perspective against our natural background. This should inculcate a proper sympathy, respect, fear, and love for the natural universe of which we are a part. And while we are helping the young people to climb that mountain from which they may look out on all the wonder and beauty of the world, we should give them the chance to loiter and day-dream a bit on the way. We can be sure then that some of their dreams will come true.

From "Science for the Good of Your Soul"
by R. L. M. Synge

1 Do you agree that our society regards education "as a machine for the mass production and training of functionaries"? What are the influences that determine the kind of education a country makes available to its citizens? Is it sufficient to define liberal education as one that promotes the will to find interests and the ability to preserve them?

2 Which of the four main kinds of scientific research mentioned by Synge would you consider to be (i) the most valuable, (ii) the most satisfying?

3 Synge seems to suggest that the satisfactions to be derived from

scientific research—the moments of exaltation, the sense of contributing one small portion to a vast cumulative endeavour, doing and completing plain hard work—could be enjoyed by a much greater number of people. Do you agree? If so, what conditions do you think are necessary to such a development?

4 What substitutes may be (or have been) discovered for the satisfaction we are alleged (or have been conditioned) to derive from "doing and completing plain hard work"?

5 Consider the arguments for and against the provision of a highly flexible education service that the individual could use how and when he chose throughout the term of his natural life.

6 Synge pleads that man should have his perspective on human life restored to him. Have the day-dreams of young people any part to play in this?

Part Five

Religious Beliefs

O world invisible, we view thee,
O world intangible, we touch thee,
O world unknowable, we know thee,
Inapprehensible, we clutch thee!

Does the fish soar to find the ocean,
The eagle plunge to find the air—
That we ask of the stars in motion
If they have rumour of thee there?

Not where the wheeling systems darken,
And our benumbed conceiving soars!—
The drift of pinions, would we hearken,
Beats at our own clay-shuttered doors.

The angels keep their ancient places;—
Turn but a stone and start a wing!
'Tis ye, 'tis your estranged faces,
That miss the many-splendoured thing.

But (when so sad thou canst not sadder)
Cry;—and upon thy so sore loss
Shall shine the traffic of Jacob's ladder
Pitched between Heaven and Charing Cross.

Yea, in the night, my Soul, my daughter,
Cry,—clinging Heaven by the hems;
And lo, Christ walking on the water
Not of Gennesareth, but Thames!

"In no Strange Land" by Francis Thompson

1 Does faith require evidence? Belief (or faith) in a supernatural power
is something that operates according to different criteria from those
that condition belief in (or acceptance of) a scientific law. Is it
possible to make a valid comparison between the two sets of criteria?

2 Is there any relationship between the thought processes that this poem
expresses and the thought processes that discovered the principle of
relativity? Is there any correspondence between the advocacy of
Thompson and Synge's plea for a "proper sympathy, respect, fear and
love for the natural universe of which we are a part"?

AN EMINENT authority has recently published a challenge to test the efficacy of prayer by actual experiment. I have been induced, through reading this, to prepare the following memoir for publication, nearly the whole of which I wrote and laid by many years ago, after completing a large collection of data, which I had undertaken for the satisfaction of my conscience.

The efficacy of prayer seems to me a simple, as it is a perfectly appropriate and legitimate, subject of scientific inquiry. Whether prayer is efficacious or not, in any given sense, is a matter of fact on which each man must form an opinion for himself. His decision will be based upon data more or less justly handled, according to his education and habits. An unscientific reasoner will be guided by a confused recollection of crude experience. A scientific reasoner will scrutinize each separate experience before he admits it as evidence, and will compare all the cases he has selected on a methodical system.

The doctrine commonly preached by the clergy is well expressed in the most recent, and by far the most temperate and learned, of theological encyclopaedias, namely, *Smith's Dictionary of the Bible*. The article on "Prayer", written by the Rev. Dr. Barry, states as follows: "Its real objective efficacy . . . is both implied and expressed (in Scripture) in the plainest terms. . . . We are encouraged to ask special blessings, both spiritual and temporal, in hopes that thus, and thus only, we may obtain them. . . . It would seem the intention of Holy Scripture to encourage all prayer, more especially intercession, in all relations and for all righteous objects." Dr. Hook, the present Dean of Chichester, states in his *Church Dictionary*, under "Prayer", that "the general providence of God acts through what are called laws of Nature. By this particular providence God interferes with those laws. . . ."

The public prayer for the sovereign of every state, Protestant and Catholic, is and has been in the spirit of our own, "Grant her in health long to live". Now, as a simple matter of fact, has this prayer any efficacy? There is a memoir by Dr. Guy, in the *Journal of the Statistical Society* (vol. xxii, p. 355), in which he compares the mean age of sovereigns with that of other classes of persons. . . . The sovereigns are literally the shortest lived of all who have the advantage of affluence. . . .

The efficacy of prayer may yet further be tested by inquiry into the proportion of deaths at the time of birth among the children of the praying and the non-praying classes. The solicitude of parents is so powerfully directed towards the safety of their expected offspring as to leave no room to doubt that pious parents pray fervently for it, especially as death before baptism is considered a most serious evil by many Christians. However, the distribution of still-births appears wholly unaffected by piety. . . .

When we pray in our Liturgy "that the nobility may be endued with grace, wisdom, and understanding", we pray for that which is clearly incompatible with insanity. Does that frightful scourge spare our nobility? Does it spare very religious people more than others? The answer is an emphatic negative to both of these questions. . . .

If prayerful habits had influence on temporal success, it is very probable, as we must again repeat, that insurance offices, of at least some descriptions, would long ago have discovered and made allowance for it. It would be most unwise, from a business point of view, to allow the devout, supposing their greater longevity even probable, to obtain annuities at the same low rates as the profane. Before insurance offices accept a life, they make confidential inquiries into the antecedents of the applicant. But such a question has never been heard of as, "Does he habitually use family prayers and private devotions?" Insurance offices, so wakeful to sanatory influences, absolutely ignore prayer as one of them. The same is true for insurances of all descriptions, as those connected with fire, ships, lightning, hail, accidental death, and cattle sickness. . . .

Nothing that I have said negatives the fact that the mind may be relieved by the utterance of prayer. The impulse to pour out the feelings in sound is not peculiar to man. Any mother that has lost her young, and wanders about moaning and looking piteously for sympathy, possesses much of that which prompts men to pray in articulate words. There is a yearning of the heart, a craving for help, it knows not where, certainly from no source that it sees. Of a similar kind is the bitter cry of the hare, when the greyhound is almost upon her; she abandons hope through her own efforts, and screams—but to whom? It is a voice convulsively sent out into space, whose utterance is a physical relief. These feelings of distress and of terror are simple, and an inarticulate cry suffices to give vent to them; but the reason why man is not satisfied by uttering inarticulate cries (though sometimes they are felt to be the most appropriate) is owing to his superior intellectual powers. His memory travels back through interlacing paths, and dwells on various connected incidents; his emotions are complex, and he prays at length.

Neither does anything I have said profess to throw light on the question of how far it is possible for man to commune in his heart with God. We know that many persons of high intellectual gifts and critical minds look upon it as an axiomatic certainty that they possess this power, although it is impossible for them to establish any satisfactory criterion to distinguish between what may really be borne in upon them from without and what arises from within, but which, through a sham of the imagination, appears to be external. A confident sense of communion with God must necessarily rejoice and strengthen the heart, and divert it from petty cares; and it is equally certain that similar benefits are not excluded from those who on conscientious grounds are sceptical as to the reality of a power of communion. These can dwell on the undoubted fact, that there exists a solidarity between themselves and what surrounds them, through the endless reactions of physical laws, among which the hereditary influences are to be included. They know that they are descended from an endless past, that they have a brotherhood with all that is, and have each his own share of responsibility in the parentage of an endless future. The effort to familiarize the imagination with this great idea has much in common with the effort of communing with a God, and its reaction on the mind of the thinker is in many important respects the same. It may not equally rejoice the heart, but it is quite as powerful in ennobling the resolves, and it is found to give serenity during the trials of life and in the shadow of approaching death.

From "Statistical Inquiries into the Efficacy of Prayer"
by Francis Galton

1 What elements in this passage are rational, what elements are emotive, and what elements are designedly persuasive?

2 Consider the reasons different people have for praying, and compare your suggestions with the three reasons proposed by Galton. Is prayer any more than a kind of spiritual day-dreaming? (And if not, how do you think R. L. M. Synge would value the activity?)

3 Galton posits two kinds of men: those who look upon it as an axiomatic certainty that they possess the power to commune in their hearts with God; and those who are sceptical as to the reality of a power of communion, but who dwell on the undoubted fact that there exists a solidarity between themselves and what surrounds them. Are these two basic attitudes opposed and mutually exclusive, or is either one inclusive of the other?

4 What are the advantages and disadvantages of drawing conclusions about human behaviour from studies of the behaviour of animals? Account for the current regard for behaviourist principles.

5 In what ways has man's proclivity for prayer been abused and taken advantage of by Church and State? Do the temporal authorities help in any way?

6 Do you agree with the argument that commonality of prayer is the best hope for the unifying of the various Christian Churches, and, indeed, for world-wide religious tolerance and understanding?

7   Have you any comment to make about the content and tone of the final sentence in the extract: "It may not equally rejoice the heart, but it is quite as powerful in ennobling the resolves, and it is found to give serenity during the trials of life and in the shadow of approaching death"?

8   Galton suggests that prayer is a palliative, a comforting self-delusion. The Christian accepts the doctrine of free will and hence of individual responsibility. From this great loneliness, what might the Christian have to say about Galton's apparent craving for solidarity with his surroundings and submersion of self? Which is the more distorted model for argument, Galton's or the one just proposed?

Now I had already collected that the mercantile affairs of the Erewhonians were conducted on a totally different system from our own; I had, however, gathered little hitherto, except that they had two distinct commercial systems, of which the one appealed more strongly to the imagination than anything to which we are accustomed in Europe, inasmuch as the banks that were conducted upon this system were decorated in the most profuse fashion, and all mercantile transactions were accompanied with music, so that they were called Musical Banks, though their music was hideous to a European ear. . .

I had long wanted to know more of this strange system, and had the greatest desire to accompany my hostess and her daughters. I had seen them go out almost every morning since my arrival and had noticed that they carried their purses in their hands, not exactly ostentatiously, yet just so as that those who met them should see whither they were going. I had never, however, yet been asked to go with them myself. . . . I was determined, however, to bring matters to an issue with my hostess about my going with them, and after a little parleying, and many inquiries as to whether I was perfectly sure that I myself wished to go, it was decided that I might do so.

We passed through several streets of more or less considerable houses, and at last turning round a corner we came upon a large piazza, at the end of which was a magnificent building, of a strange but novel architecture and of great antiquity. It did not open directly on to the piazza, there being a screen, through which was an archway, between the piazza and the actual precincts of the bank. On passing under the archway we entered upon a green sward. . . .

We crossed the sward and entered the building. If the outside had been impressive the inside was even more so. It was very lofty and divided into several parts by walls which rested upon massive pillars; the windows were filled with stained glass descriptive of the principal commercial incidents of the bank for many ages. In a remote part of the building there were men and boys singing. . . . As soon as the singing was over, the ladies requested me to stay where I was while they went inside the place from which it had seemed to come.

During their absence certain reflections forced themselves upon me.

In the first place, it struck me as strange that the building should be so nearly empty; I was almost alone, and the few besides myself had been led by curiosity, and had no intention of doing business with the bank. But there might be more inside. I stole up to the curtain and ventured to draw the extreme edge of it on one side. No, there was hardly anyone there. I saw a large number of cashiers, all at their desks ready to pay cheques, and one or two who seemed to be the managing partners. I also saw my hostess and her daughters and two or three other ladies; also three or four old women and the boys from one of the neighbouring Colleges of Unreason; but there was no one else. This did not look as though the bank was doing a very large business; and yet I had always been told that everyone in the city dealt with this establishment.

I cannot describe all that took place in these inner precincts, for a sinister-looking person in a black gown came and made unpleasant gestures at me for peeping. I happened to have in my pocket one of the musical bank pieces, which had been given me by Mrs. Nosnibor, so I tried to tip him with it; but having seen what it was, he became so angry that I had to give him a piece of the other kind of money to pacify him. When I had done this he became civil directly. As soon as he was gone I ventured to take a second look, and saw Zulora in the very act of giving a piece of paper which looked like a cheque to one of the cashiers. He did not examine it, but putting his hand into an antique coffer hard by, he pulled out a quantity of metal pieces apparently at random, and handed them over without counting them; neither did Zulora count them but put them into her purse and went back to her seat after dropping a few pieces of the other coinage into an alms-box that stood by the cashier's side. Mrs. Nosnibor and Arowhena then did likewise, but a little later they gave all (so far as I could see) that they had received from the cashier back to a verger, who I have no doubt put it back into the coffer from which it had been taken. They then began making towards the curtain; whereon I let it drop and retreated to a reasonable distance.

They soon joined me. For some few minutes we all kept silence, but at last I ventured to remark that the bank was not so busy today as it probably often was. On this Mrs. Nosnibor said that it was indeed melancholy to see what little heed people paid to the most precious of all institutions. . . .

Mrs. Nosnibor went on to say that I must not think there was any want of confidence in the bank because I had seen so few people there; the heart of the country was thoroughly devoted to these establishments. . . .

She might say what she pleased, but her manner carried no conviction and later on I saw signs of general indifference to these banks that were not to be mistaken. Their supporters often denied it, but the denial was generally so couched as to add another proof of its existence. In commercial panics and in times of general distress, the people as a mass did not so much as even think of turning to these banks. A few might do so, some from habit and early training, some from the instinct that prompts us to catch at any straw when we think ourselves drowning, but few from a genuine belief that the Musical Banks could save them from financial ruin if they were able to meet their engagements in the other kind of currency.

In conversation with one of the musical bank managers I ventured to hint this as plainly as politeness would allow. He said that it had been more or less true till lately, but that now they had put stained glass windows into all the banks in the country, and repaired the buildings, and enlarged the organs; the presidents, moreover, had taken to riding in omnibuses and talking nicely to people in the streets, and to remembering the ages of their children, and giving them things when they were naughty so that all would henceforth go smoothly.

"But haven't you done anything to the money itself?" said I, timidly.

"It is not necessary," he rejoined; "not in the least necessary, I assure you".

From *Erewhon* by Samuel Butler

1 What is the point of this allegory? What is the Bank, and who are the people? And what is the real nature of the transaction between Zulora and the cashier?

2 Allegorists and satirists have the didactic advantage of being able to select those elements in a total situation that most readily lend themselves to praise or ridicule. Is truth thus surrendered to persuasion? As long as ideas and interpretations circulate freely, does it matter?

3 The world, some say, is divided into those who have to be looked after and those who do the looking after. A modern division might be between those who do and those who disparage. Is each absolutely necessary to the other?

WILL YOU see the infancy of this sublime and celestial greatness?
Those pure and virgin apprehensions I had in my infancy, and that
divine light wherewith I was born, are the best unto this day wherein
I can see the universe. By the gift of God they attended me into the
world, and by His special favour I remember them till now. Verily
they form the greatest gifts His wisdom could bestow, for without
them all other gifts had been dead and vain. They are unattainable by
books, and therefore I will teach them by experience. Pray for them
earnestly, for they will make you angelical and wholly celestial.
Certainly Adam in Paradise had not more sweet and curious apprehensions of the world than I when I was a child.

All appeared new and strange at first, inexpressibly rare and
delightful and beautiful. I was a little stranger which at my entrance
into the world was saluted and surrounded with innumerable joys.
My knowledge was Divine; I knew by intuition those things which
since my apostacy I collected again by the highest reason. My very
ignorance was advantageous. I seemed as one brought into the estate
of innocence. All things were spotless and pure and glorious; yea,
and infinitely mine and joyful and precious. I knew not that there
were any sins, or complaints or law. I dreamed not of poverties,
contentions, or views. All tears and quarrels were hidden from mine
eyes. Everything was at rest, free and immortal. I knew nothing of
sickness or death or exaction. In the absence of these I was entertained
like an angel with the works of God in their splendour and glory; I
saw all in the peace of Eden; heaven and earth did sing my Creator's
praises, and could not make more melody to Adam than to me.
All time was Eternity, and a perpetual Sabbath. Is it not strange that
an infant should be heir of the whole world, and see those mysteries
which the books of the learned never unfold?

The corn was orient and immortal wheat which never should be
reaped nor was ever sown. I thought it had stood from everlasting to
everlasting. The dust and stones of the street were as precious as
gold: the gates were at first the end of the world. The green trees
when I saw them first through one of the gates transported and
ravished me; their sweetness and unusual beauty made my heart to
leap, and almost mad with ecstasy, they were such strange and wonderful things. The Men! O what venerable and reverend creatures did the
aged seem! Immortal Cherubims! And young men glittering and
sparkling angels, and maids strange seraphic pieces of life and beauty!
Boys and girls tumbling in the street were moving jewels: I knew
not that they were born or should die. But all things abided eternally
as they were in their proper places. Eternity was manifest in the
Light of the Day, and something infinite behind everything appeared,
which talked with my expectation and moved my desire. The City

seemed to stand in Eden or to be built in Heaven. The streets were mine, the temple was mine, the people were mine, their clothes and gold and silver were mine, as much as their sparkling eyes, fair skins, and ruddy faces. The skies were mine, and so were the sun and moon and stars, and all the world was mine; and I the only spectator and enjoyer of it. I knew no churlish proprieties, nor bounds nor divisions; but all properties and divisions were mine, all treasures and the possessors of them. So that with much ado I was corrupted, and made to learn the dirty devices of this world, which now I unlearn, and become, as it were, a little child again that I may enter into the Kingdom of God.

From *Centuries of Meditation* by Thomas Traherne

1   Wordsworth echoed Traherne's valuation of his childhood : "Heaven shone about me in my infancy" and "The child is father of the man". Were these two men justified in making so much of the excitement and wonder that naturally attends upon a child's first explorations of an unfamiliar world ? After all, even as an adult, one's sensibilities are heightened during one's first day in a foreign city.

2   Do children know no "dirty devices" ? When does one begin to acquire a moral sense ? Is Traherne proposing to trade in such painfully learned virtues as charity and resolution for a bit of heightened sensibility ?

3   What is Traherne really saying ? How would you describe the state of innocence he longs for ?

4   The vision of a mystic—the vision of a child. Because these visions are rare in incidence or short in duration, are they any less real or significant ?

5   What is common to the thought of Thompson, Galton, and Traherne ?

THE DIFFICULTY in approaching the question of the relations between Religion and Science is, that its elucidation requires that we have in our minds some clear idea of what we mean by either of the terms, "religion" and "science". Also I wish to speak in the most general way possible, and to keep in the background any comparison of particular creeds, scientific or religious. We have got to understand the type of connection which exists between the two spheres, and then to draw some definite conclusions respecting the existing situation which at present confronts the world.

The *conflict* between religion and science is what naturally occurs

4

to our minds when we think of this subject. It seems as though, during the last half-century, the results of science and the beliefs of religion had come into a position of frank disagreement, from which there can be no escape, except by abandoning either the clear teaching of science, or the clear teaching of religion. This conclusion has been urged by controversialists on either side. Not by all controversialists, of course, but by those trenchant intellects which every controversy calls out into the open.

The distress of sensitive minds, and the zeal for truth, and the sense of the importance of the issues, must command our sincerest sympathy. When we consider what religion is for mankind, and what science is, it is no exaggeration to say that the future course of history depends upon the decision of this generation as to the relations between them. We have here the two strongest general forces (apart from the mere impulse of the various senses) which influence men, and they seem to be set one against the other—the force of our religious intuitions, and the force of our impulse to accurate observation and logical deduction.

A great English statesman once advised his countrymen to use large-scale maps, as a preservative against alarms, panics, and general misunderstanding of the true relations between nations. In the same way in dealing with the clash between permanent elements of human nature, it is well to map our history on a large scale, and to disengage ourselves from our immediate absorption in the present conflicts. When we do this, we immediately discover two great facts. In the first place, there has always been a conflict between religion and science; and in the second place, both religion and science have always been in a state of continual development. In the early days of Christianity, there was a general belief among Christians that the world was coming to an end in the lifetime of people then living. We can make only indirect inferences as to how far this belief was authoritatively proclaimed; but it is certain that it was widely held, and that it formed an impressive part of the popular religious doctrine. The belief proved itself to be mistaken, and Christian doctrine adjusted itself to the change. Again in the early Church individual theologians very confidently deduced from the Bible opinions concerning the nature of the physical universe. In the year A.D. 535, a monk named Cosmas wrote a book which he entitled *Christian Topography*. He was a travelled man who had visited India and Ethiopia; and finally he lived in a monastery at Alexandria, which was then a great centre of culture. In this book, basing himself upon the direct meaning of Biblical texts as construed by him in a literal fashion, he denied the existence of the antipodes, and asserted that the world is a flat parallelogram whose length is double its breadth.

In the seventeenth century the doctrine of the motion of the earth was condemned by a Catholic tribunal. A hundred years ago the extension of time demanded by geological science distressed religious people, Protestant and Catholic. And today the doctrine of evolution is an equal stumbling-block. These are only a few instances illustrating a general fact.

But all our ideas will be in a wrong perspective if we think that this recurring perplexity was confined to contradictions between religion and science; and that in these controversies religion was always wrong, and that science was always right. The true facts of the case are very much more complex, and refuse to be summarized in these simple terms.

Theology itself exhibits exactly the same character of gradual development, arising from an aspect of conflict between its own proper ideas. This fact is a commonplace to theologians, but is often obscured in the stress of controversy. I do not wish to overstate my case; so I will confine myself to Roman Catholic writers. In the seventeenth century a learned Jesuit, Father Petavius, showed that the theologians of the first three centuries of Christianity made use of phrases and statements which since the fifth century would be condemned as heretical. Also Cardinal Newman devoted a treatise to the discussion of the development of doctrine. He wrote it before he became a great Roman Catholic ecclesiastic; but throughout his life it was never retracted and continually reissued.

Science is even more changeable than theology. No man of science could subscribe without qualification to Galileo's beliefs, or to Newton's beliefs, or to all his own scientific beliefs of ten years ago.

In both regions of thought, additions, distinctions, and modifications have been introduced. So that now, even when the same assertion is made today as was made a thousand, or fifteen hundred years ago, it is made subject to limitations or expansions of meaning, which were not contemplated at the earlier epoch. We are told by logicians that a proposition must be either true or false, and that there is no middle term. But in practice, we may know that a proposition expresses an important truth, but that it is subject to limitations and qualifications which at present remain undiscovered. It is a general feature of our knowledge, that we are insistently aware of important truths; and yet that the only formulations of these truths which we are able to make presuppose a general standpoint of conceptions which may have to be modified. I will give you two illustrations, both from science : Galileo said that the earth moves and that the sun is fixed; the Inquisition said that the earth is fixed and the sun moves; and Newtonian astronomers, adopting an absolute theory of space, said that both the sun and the earth move. But now we say that any one of these three statements are equally true, provided that you have fixed your sense of "rest" and "motion" in the way required by the statement adopted. At the date of Galileo's controversy with the Inquisition, Galileo's way of stating the facts was, beyond question, the fruitful procedure for the sake of scientific research. But in itself it was not more true than the formulation of the Inquisition. But at that time the modern concepts of relative motion were in nobody's mind; so that the statements were made in ignorance of the qualifications required for their more perfect truth. Yet this question of the motions of the earth and the sun expresses a real fact in the universe; and all sides had got hold of important truths concerning it. But with the knowledge of those times, the truths appeared to be inconsistent.

Again I will give you another example taken from the state of modern physical science. Since the time of Newton and Huygens in the seventeenth century there have been two theories as to the physical nature of light. Newton's theory was that a beam of light consists of a stream of very minute particles, or corpuscles, and that we have the sensation of light when these corpuscles strike the retinas of our eyes. Huygens' theory was that light consists of very minute waves of trembling in an all-pervading ether, and that these waves are travelling along a beam of light. The two theories are contradictory. In the eighteenth century Newton's theory was believed, in the nineteenth century Huygens' theory was believed. Today there is one large group of phenomena which can be explained only on the wave theory, and another large group which can be explained only on the corpuscular theory. Scientists have to leave it at that, and wait for the future, in the hope of attaining some wider vision which reconciles both.

We should apply these same principles to the questions in which there is a variance between science and religion. We would believe nothing in either sphere of thought which does not appear to us to be certified by solid reasons based upon the critical research either of ourselves or of competent authorities. But granting that we have honestly taken this precaution, a clash between the two on points of detail where they overlap should not lead us hastily to abandon doctrines for which we have solid evidence. It may be that we are more interested in one set of doctrines than in the other. But, if we have any sense of perspective and of the history of thought, we shall wait and refrain from mutual anathemas.

From *Science and the Modern World*
by A. N. Whitehead.

1 A. N. Whitehead delivered the address from which this extract is taken in 1925. What has happened since then to confirm, modify, or deny his statement "it is no exaggeration to say that the future course of history

depends upon the decision of this generation as to the relations between them" (religion and science).

2 Whitehead claims that religion and science are "the two strongest general forces (apart from the mere impulse of the various senses) which influence men". What other influential "general forces" might dispute this claim?

3 What elements of religion are at critical stages of development in the present decade? What changes in man's knowledge or in society have stimulated such developments? Are any religious tenets sacrosanct? How do you account for the continued and clamant existence of certain fundamental sects.

4 "No man of science could subscribe without qualification—to all his own scientific beliefs of ten years ago." What are the implications for scientists and educators? Does science proceed in the main by slight modifications of doubtful assertions? Is a scientist a fool to become a "martyr for truth"?

5 Give present-day instances where a conflict of ideas has degenerated into "mutual anathemas". Is it possible to guard against such waste of productive thinking?

6 Whitehead seems to invoke the theory of relativity to justify changes in religious beliefs, as well as modifications of scientific understanding. He is intent upon establishing a significant likeness between religion and science by examining the nature of their development. What other aspects of the two activities remain to be examined?

Part Six

Moral Responsibility

THE SUDDEN changing of Mrs. Tebrick into a vixen is an established fact which we may attempt to account for as we will. Certainly it is in the explanation of the fact, and the reconciling of it with our general notions that we shall find most difficulty, and not in accepting for true a story which is so fully proved, and that not by one witness but by a dozen, all respectable, and with no possibility of collusion between them. . . .

A grown lady is changed straightway into a fox. There is no explaining that away by any natural philosophy. The materialism of our age will not help us here. It is indeed a miracle; something from outside our world altogether; an event which we would willingly accept if we were to meet it invested with the authority of Divine Revelation in the scriptures, but which we are not prepared to encounter almost in our time, happening in Oxfordshire amongst our neighbours. . . .

On one of the first days of the year 1880, in the early afternoon, husband and wife went for a walk in the copse on the hill above Rylands. . . .

Hearing the hunt, Mr. Tebrick quickened his pace so as to reach the edge of the copse, where they might get a good view of the hounds if they came that way. His wife hung back, and he, holding her hand, began almost to drag her. Before they gained the edge of the copse she suddenly snatched her hand away from his very violently and cried out, so that he instantly turned his head.

Where his wife had been the moment before was a small fox, of a very bright red. It looked at him very beseechingly, advanced towards him a pace or two, and he saw at once that his wife was looking at him from the animal's eyes. You may well think if he were aghast: and so maybe was his lady at finding herself in that shape, so they did nothing for nearly half-an-hour but stare at each other, he bewildered, she asking him with her eyes as if indeed she spoke to him: "What am I now become? Have pity on me, husband, have pity on me for I am your wife. . . ."

When it was dark he brought her in with infinite precautions, yet not without the dogs scenting her, after which nothing could moderate their clamour.

Having got her into the house, the next thing he thought of was to hide her from the servants. He carried her to the bedroom in his arms and then went downstairs again. . . .

The next morning he looked about him at the place and found the thing there that he most wanted, and that was a little walled-in garden where his wife could run in freedom and yet be in safety.

After they had had breakfast she was wild to go out into the snow. So they went out together, and he had never seen such a mad creature

in all his life as his wife was then. For she ran to and fro as if she were
crazy, biting at the snow and rolling in it, and round and round in
circles and rushed back at him fiercely as if she meant to bite him.
He joined her in the frolic, and began snowballing her till she was so
wild that it was all he could do to quiet her again and bring her
indoors for luncheon. Indeed with her gambollings she tracked the
whole garden over with her feet; he could see where she had rolled in
the snow and where she had danced in it, and looking at those prints
of her feet as they went in, made his heart ache, he knew not
why. . . .

Then he got up quickly and went to the door of the garden that
opened into a little paddock against a wood.

When he opened it she went through like an arrow, crossed the
paddock like a puff of smoke and in a moment was gone from his
sight. Then, suddenly finding himself alone, Mr. Tebrick came as it
were to himself and ran after her, calling her by name and shouting to
her, and so went plunging into the wood, and through it for about a
mile, running almost blindly. . . .

That night he slept indoors, but in the morning early he was
awoken by the sound of trotting horses and running to the window
saw a farmer riding by very sprucely dressed. Could they be hunting so
soon, he wondered, but presently reassured himself that it could not
be a hunt already.

He heard no other sound till eleven o'clock in the morning when
suddenly there was the clamour of hounds giving tongue and not so
far off either. At this Mr. Tebrick ran out of his house distracted and
set open the gates of his garden, but with iron bars and wire at the
top so the huntsmen could not follow. There was silence again; it
seems the fox must have turned away, for there was no other sound
of the hunt. Mr. Tebrick was now like one helpless with fear, he
dared not go out, yet could not stay still at home. There was nothing
that he could do, yet he would not admit this, so he busied himself in
making holes in the hedges, so that Silvia could enter from whatever
side she came. . . .

Now it was that poor Mr. Tebrick made his great mistake, for
hearing the hounds almost outside the gate he ran to meet them,
whereas rightly he should have run back to the house. As soon as he
reached the gate he saw his wife Silvia coming towards him but very
tired with running and just upon her the hounds. . . .

His vixen had at once sprung into Mr. Tebrick's arms, and before
he could turn back the hounds were upon them and had pulled them
down. Then at that moment there was a scream of despair heard
by all the field that had come up, which they declared afterwards
was more like a woman's voice than a man's. But yet there was no

clear proof whether it was Mr. Tebrick or his wife who had suddenly regained her voice.

From *Lady into Fox* by David Garnett

1 Francis Bacon wrote, "He who hath wife and children hath given hostages to fortune." Fortune certainly put Mr. Tebrick's sense of responsibility and personal adequacy to the test! Why are men and women capable of such sacrifices for each other or for their children?

2 What responsibilities has man for animal life? Do you draw the line at vivisection, blood sports, medical experiments, battery rearing, the Sunday joint, cruelty or neglect? Is it right that this country should spend more on feeding its dogs than it spends on aid to under-developed countries where people are starving?

3 Do you agree with the author's assertion that we are prepared to accept miracles (or to recognize that some events are inexplicable) only if they happened a long time ago? Is the general ridicule of the Flying Saucer believers sensible—or is it unwise, or arrogant, or even immoral?

4 "Mary—I want my freedom!" How often have we heard some such desperate request made in films and plays. Under what circumstances has a man or a woman the right to ask for such release from responsibility; and what considerations should govern the reply?

IT IS not enough that a practitioner should have had a single case of puerperal fever not followed by others. It must be known whether he attended others while this case was in progress, whether he went directly from one chamber to others, whether he took any, and what, precautions. It is important to know that several women were exposed to infection derived from the patient, so that allowance may be made for want of predisposition. Now, if of negative facts so sifted there could be accumulated a hundred for every one plain instance of communication here recorded, I trust it need not be said that we are bound to guard and watch over the hundredth tenant of our fold, though the ninety and nine may be sure of escaping the wolf at its entrance. If anyone is disposed, then, to take a hundred instances of lives, endangered or sacrificed out of those I have mentioned, and make it reasonably clear that within a similar time and compass ten thousand escaped the same exposure, I shall thank him for his industry, but I must be permitted to hold to my own practical conclusions, and beg him to adopt or at least to examine them also. Children that walk in calico before open fires are not always burned to death; the instances to the contrary may be worth recording; but by no means if they are to be used as arguments against woollen frocks and high fenders. . . .

The practical point to be illustrated is the following: the disease known as puerperal fever is so far contagious as to be frequently carried from patient to patient by physicians and nurses. . . .

The recurrence of long series of cases like those I have cited, reported by those most interested to disbelieve in contagion, scattered along through an interval of half a century, might have been thought sufficient to satisfy the minds of all inquirers that here was something more than a singular coincidence. But if, on a more extended observation, it should be found that the same omenous groups of cases clustering about individual practitioners were observed in a remote country, at different times, and in widely separated regions, it would seem incredible that any should be found too prejudiced or indolent to accept the solemn truth knelled into their ears by the funeral bells from both sides of the ocean—the plain conclusion that the physician and the disease entered, hand in hand, into the chamber of the unsuspecting patient. . . .

Now add to all this the undisputed fact that within the walls of lying-in hospitals there is often generated a miasma, palpable as the chlorine used to destroy it, tenacious so as in some cases almost to defy extirpation, deadly in some institutions as the plague; which has killed women in a private hospital of London so fast that they were buried two in one coffin to conceal its horrors; which enabled Tonnelle to record 222 autopsies at the Maternité of Paris; which has led Dr. Lee to express his deliberate conviction that the loss of life occasioned by these institutions completely defeats the objects of their founders; and out of this train of cumulative evidence, the multiplied groups of cases clustering about individuals, the deadly results of autopsies, the inoculation by fluids from the living patient, the murderous poison of hospitals—does there not result a conclusion that laughs all sophistry to scorn, and renders all argument an insult? . . .

I have no wish to express any harsh feeling with regard to the painful subject which has come before us. If there are any so far excited by the story of these dreadful events that they ask for some word of indignant remonstrance to show that science does not turn the hearts of its followers into ice or stone, let me remind them that such words have been uttered by those who speak with an authority I could not claim. It is as a lesson rather than as a reproach that I call up the memory of these irreparable errors and wrongs. No tongue can tell the heartbreaking calamity they have caused; they have closed the eyes just opened upon a new world of love and happiness; they have bowed the strength of manhood into the dust; they have cast the helplessness of infancy into the stranger's arms, or bequeathed it, with less cruelty, the death of its dying parent. There is no tone deep enough for regret, and no voice loud enough for warning. The woman about to become a mother, or with her newborn infant upon her bosom, should be the object of trembling care and sympathy wherever she bears her tender burden or stretches her aching limbs. The very outcast of the streets has pity upon her sister in degradation when the seal of promised maternity is impressed upon her. The remorseless vengeance of the law, brought down upon its victim by a machinery as sure as destiny, is arrested in its fall at a word which reveals her transient claim for mercy. The solemn prayer of the liturgy singles out her sorrows from the multiplied trials of life, to plead for her in the hour of peril. God forbid that any member of the profession to which she trusts her life, doubly precious at that eventful period, should hazard it negligently, unadvisedly, or selfishly! . . .

Whatever indulgence may be granted to those who have heretofore been the ignorant causes of so much misery, the time has come when the existence of a private pestilence in the sphere of a single physician should be looked upon, not as a misfortune, but a crime; and in the knowledge of such occurrences the duties of the practitioner to his profession should give way to his paramount obligations to society.

From "The Contagiousness of Puerperal Fever"
by Oliver Wendell Holmes

1 Why would the majority of people rather preserve habit (smoking, drinking before driving, working with a heavy cold) than preserve life? Has a democratically elected government the right and the duty to break the injurious habits of the majority that elected it?

2 What evidence is there that the health authorities are now acting on the principle that prevention is better than cure? How have the authorities tried to educate the public in this regard?

3 What are the distinguishing features of "a profession"? Would you agree that the fundamental requirement is the individual exercise of direct responsibility for the lives and well-being of others? Or has it something to do with discipline? Or decision-making?

4 A pregnant woman carries two lives and usually attracts sympathy, concern, forbearance. But do all people who are at risk or in misfortune get the attention they deserve? And do others get more than their fair share? Why?

5 Should a teacher reveal the misconduct (petty larceny) of his colleague and destroy his career, if that colleague happens to be a conscientious,

unusually gifted teacher? Recall or invent situations in which men in various professions have had to decide a conflict of duties or responsibilities, a conflict that has arisen out of the very nature of their work.

MY LORD, I am now to have the honour of placing in your hands the document which confers upon you the freedom of this ancient city, to mark our high appreciation of those successful efforts which, with untiring devotion during a long life, you have made to ameliorate the moral and physical condition of the labouring classes, and in recognition generally of the work which you have performed as a Christian philanthropist. One of the first great movements to which you devoted yourself after entering Parliament as Lord Ashley was that for the reduction of the hours of labour for children and young persons in the cotton and other mills of the country. The moral and physical evils of the system which then prevailed were of such a character that, viewed from the time in which we live, seems hardly credible. The daily hours of labour during which children of tender years of both sexes were compelled to work in factories were so prolonged that their health was impaired and their lives shortened; and they were, besides, not infrequently subjected to cruel treatment at the hands of those set over them. In some mills, children walked in a day, while accomplishing their task, a distance of thirty miles, which your lordship truly described in your place in Parliament as a labour more severe than that imposed on soldiers in forced marches, or under arms before an enemy. In such circumstances, the possibility of their getting anything better than the most meagre education was utterly hopeless. This great movement for the reduction of the hours of labour began in the year 1830, but Mr. Sadler, one of its most zealous and eloquent advocates, lost his seat in the next Parliament. It was then, my lord, in 1833, that you espoused the cause of those oppressed children, by introducing your Ten Hours Bill. The Government declined to accept its most important part, but, feeling that humanity demanded a change, passed a measure in which they granted some concessions, including the great principle that education and labour should go together. Your lordship's eloquent and powerful pleadings on behalf of these operatives, that their hours of labour should be restricted, were received in the most hostile manner. Manufacturers, supposing that their profits would be seriously lessened by such a change, gave your Bill the most determined opposition; and a portion of the Press advocated their views. Nearly all the leading statesmen of the time, whatever their politics, were also against the ten hours' principle, and successive Governments declined to accept it. But, my lord, strong in the righteousness of your cause, and nothing daunted, you continued your work of mercy. The measure which the Government had passed was allowed to become practically inoperative, and they declined or delayed to take further action. Discontent began to arise in the manufacturing districts. A tremendous evil existed. The children of the poor continued to be oppressed for the further aggrandisement of the rich. . . . Through long years, amidst much obloquy, you fought the battle until the victory was gained. And when your lordship visited the manufacturing districts after this great work was accomplished, the enthusiastic ovation which greeted you showed how much your labours were appreciated by those immediately concerned; and I am sure it must be a source of supreme satisfaction to your lordship now to know that all the classes of the community cheerfully acknowledge the wisdom and beneficence of the measure you were instrumental in getting passed into law. In 1840, when the principle of the ten hours' limit for the labours of factory children had been accepted by the country, although a law enacting it had not been passed by the Government, you proceeded towards carrying out the next part of your work. Accordingly, you succeeded in getting a royal commission appointed to inquire into the employment of children in mines and collieries, and in various branches of trade and manufacture in which numbers of children worked together. Regarding collieries and mines—to which I shall only refer—the commission revealed facts which filled the public mind with horror and indignation. Children—infants, I should say—of only four or five years of age were made to toil in the mines in a manner which was a disgrace to humanity, while women laboured at employment degrading to their sex. Young children, girls as well as boys, were made to draw loads by a chain and girdle through places so narrow that they had to pass on all fours; and the regular hours of work for children were from eleven to thirteen a day, and sometimes more. Six months' labour in the mines was sufficient to effect a very visible change on their appearance, and the baneful results of the system upon their constitution could not well be exaggerated. Notwithstanding the facts brought to light by the commissioners, the time had not arrived when such extensive changes as were required could be effected, but ultimately a bill was passed which altogether prohibited females from working underground, and no boys under a specified age were permitted to be employed. . . . Your labours also in the cause of education, and as chairman of the Ragged School Union—over which you have presided since its formation four-and-thirty years ago—have left a great mark upon the country. . . . But further let me say, that among the many benevolent institutions which your lordship has originated, the National Refuges for Homeless and Destitute Children, and the training-ships *Chichester* and *Arethusa*, take a prominent place. . . . Your lordship's position in connection with the British and Foreign Bible Society stands out so prominently, that to it I must make a passing allusion. You have been the president of that important institution for the last twenty-seven years, and have always been present at its annual gatherings in Exeter Hall. . . . The course of your life all through has been the unselfish promotion of the well-being of others. Nor, as we have seen, have you confined yourself to your own country. Not only has your eye of pity fallen upon the ragged and deserted child of the street, but the enslaved son of Africa has also elicited your commiseration, and from them upwards through the social scale you have sought to do good to all. The records of those religious and benevolent societies to which I have referred show that your charity extended to all lands, and that the aspiration of your soul was that the time might speedily come when the grace of God would regenerate all men. Permit me to say that you have lived a noble life, have accomplished a noble work, and will leave behind you a noble example.

> From a speech of Mr. T. J. Boyd, Lord Provost of Edinburgh,
> when bestowing the freedom of the city
> on the Earl of Shaftesbury in 1878

1   It is difficult nowadays to reconcile the brutality of working conditions in the mines and mills of early nineteenth-century England with the high incidence of religious observance and the pre-eminent position of the nation. In what respects has the public conscience become more tender, and in what respects more callous? What might appear as irreconcilable features of mid-twentieth century life to the mid-twenty-first century observer?

2   Are social reforms the outcome of the work of dedicated individuals, the accumulation of grievance or the recognition of that grievance? Or are they the product of these factors and some others?

3   ". . . the unselfish promotion of the well-being of others." How might a contemporary Shaftesbury earn such a commendation? What might he set his hand to and how might he do this work effectively?

4   Has every individual responsibility for the well-being of others? Can education promote understanding and the will to help without resorting to indoctrination?

IN 1813 Stephen Grellet visited Newgate prison in London. "When I first entered," he wrote, "the foulness of the air was almost insupportable; and everything that is base and depraved was so strongly depicted on the faces of the women that, for a while, my soul was greatly dismayed". He went on up to the infirmary: "I was astonished beyond description at the mass of woe and misery I beheld. I found many very sick, lying on the bare floor or on some old straw, having very scanty covering over them, and there were several children almost naked. On leaving that abode of wretchedness and misery, I went to Mildred's Court to my much valued friend Elizabeth J. Fry, to whom I described, out of the fullness of my heart, what I had just beheld. . . . She immediately sent for several pieces of flannel and had speedily collected a number of our young women Friends who went to work with such diligence, that on the very next day, she repaired to the prison with a bundle of made-up garments for the naked children. What she then saw of the wretchedness of that prison induced her to devise some plan towards the amelioration of the conditions of those poor women, and if possible, the reform of their morals and instilling into their minds the principles and love of the Christian religion. . . ."

On February 27th, 1818, Mr. Alderman Wood, a member of the committee, questioned Mrs. Fry as to the beginnings and nature of her work. "It is rather more than a year," she told him, "since I first established a school for the children of the convicts." She went on to describe the conditions and how far work was always done with the consent of the women. "They knit from about 60 to 100 pairs of stockings and socks every month; they spin a little. The earnings of their work, we think, average about eighteen pence per week for each person. Another very important point is the excellent effect we have found to result from religious education; our habit is constantly to read the Scriptures to them twice a day; it has had an astonishing effect. . . ."

One friend of Mrs. Fry's records a visit that he paid in order to see for himself what was being accomplished. "I went and requested permission to see Mrs. Fry, which was shortly obtained, and I was conducted by a turn-key to the entrance of the women's ward. On my approach, no loud or dissonant sounds or angry voices indicated that I was about to enter a place which I was credibly assured, had long had for one of its titles that of 'Hell above Ground'. The court-yard into which I was admitted, instead of being peopled with beings scarcely human, blaspheming, fighting, tearing each others' hair or gaming with a filthy pack of cards for the very clothes they wore, which often did not suffice even for decency, present⸍ l a scene where stillness and propriety reigned. I was conducted by a decently dressed person, the newly-appointed yard-woman, to the door of the ward where, at the head of a long table, sat a lady belonging to the Society of Friends. She was reading aloud to about 16 women prisoners who were engaged in needlework around it. Each wore a clean-looking blue apron and bib. They all rose on my entrance, curtsied respectfully and then, at a signal given, resumed their seats and their employments. I afterwards visited the other wards which were counterparts of the first. . . ."

Sidney Smith had strong criticisms of the introduction of classes for reading and writing in various gaols. "We enter our decided protest against these modes of occupation," he wrote, "we would banish all the looms of Preston jail, and substitute nothing but the treadwheel, or the capstan, or some species of labour where the labourer could not see the results of his toil,—where it was as monotonous, irksome, and dull as possible,—pulling and pushing instead of reading and writing,—no share of the profits—not a single shilling. There should be no tea or sugar,—no assemblage of female felons round the washing-tub, nothing but heating hemp, and pulling oakum, and pounding bricks,—no work but what was tedious, unusual, and unfeminine. Man, woman, boy, and girl should all leave the jail, unimpaired indeed in health, but heartily wearied of their residence; and taught, by sad experience, to consider it the greatest misfortune of their lives to return to it. We have the strongest belief that the present lenity of jails, the education carried on there—the cheerful assemblage of workmen—the indulgence in diet—the shares of earnings enjoyed by prisoners, are one great cause of the astonishingly rapid increase of commitments. . . ."

In 1818, women were still transferred from prison to the hulks in open wagons, but Mrs. Fry prevailed on the Governor of Newgate to send them in hackney coaches. She promised the women that if they were orderly, she would accompany them to Deptford and see them on board. She organized a classification system according to age and criminality, and business houses provided materials for patch-work and fancy-work. She had as an indefatigable helper a Mrs. Pryor, who, from 1818 to 1841, visited almost every convict ship.

Women often arrived in a deplorable condition with quite insufficient clothing. In 1822, Mrs. Pryor complained that "the prisoners from Lancaster Castle arrived, not merely handcuffed but with heavy irons on their legs, which had occasioned considerable swelling, and in one instance, serious inflammation". When women arrived in irons on board the *Brothers* in 1823, Mrs. Fry had a list taken. From this it appears that 12 arrived handcuffed; 11 from Lancaster were "iron hooped round their legs and arms and chained to each other".

From *The British Penal System* by R. S. E. Hinde

1 Restraint, retribution, and deterrence were the sole principles on which penal codes were based until comparatively recently. What new principles determine our treatment of offenders?

2 Is criminality a disease with social, psychological, or genetic origins, or is it a freely determined disposition to do evil?
Are criminals men who have not learned how to control the capacity for criminality that lodges in every man?

3 Whatever the conditions, what is the worst single feature of prison life? What is the most difficult challenge the man released from prison must face? How can he best be helped to meet it?

4 In recent years, the criminal has seemed to receive more sympathy than his victim. Can you account for this apparent perversity?
Should the person convicted of crimes of violence be made to compensate his victim financially through his work in prison?

5 Would you, in all circumstances, go to the help of a person you saw being attacked?

FEW OF us have been spared the ridiculous performances in the clinical theatres of our medical schools, where the consultant, with characteristic subtlety, orders the frail patient dressed only in gown and pants to "drop 'em and show us your scrotum". There you stand, but for the grace of God, your scrotum in his hand, in front of scores of unidentified onlookers. A monstrous situation. Surely there is hardly an adult, in possession of his senses, who hasn't some formed attitude to his or her genitalia. The interest of a case of tuberculous epididymitis seems to transcend the demands of good manners. The pathologist may then make an esoteric remark and throw the assembly into convulsions of laughter and the nightmare is complete.

When the operating-list is changed and the patient's operation delayed, it frequently happens that he is the last to hear of it, when the nurse unexpectedly brings in his breakfast. "So O.K., the patient has his operation tomorrow instead, what does it matter?" Major surgery is a commonplace to the doctor, but for the patient an operation is a singular event, often unprecedented and always evoking fear. Whilst awake the patient must surely trust implicitly in the integrity of the surgeon. Whilst he is under the anaesthetic it is of no importance if the theatre staff discusses stock-market prices, world-cup results, hospital gossip, tell jokes, or even talk about the patient when nothing else will do.

Obstetricians seem to make a virtue of exposure. I have seen departments where screens are not drawn during pelvic examination because "Mr. So-and-so doesn't like it". Patients bend the neck and submit to the law of the cow-shed; and students in attendance learn that this is the way things are done.

Academics too have their vices. They are frequently guilty of proceeding with quantifying investigations and intervention quite immaterial to prognosis when clearly they are only contributing to the anguish of the final hours. They present as justification the untenable view that from measurements obtained, further knowledge will be available for greater success in subsequent cases. This sounds grand, encompassing everything on a vast canvas, but it is achieved only by the expulsion of the individual from the universe we seek to create. Here is the essence of the duality of our experience, the conflict of "humanity" with "man as an individual"; the confrontation of medicine as a science and medicine as an art.

The mortality-rate in life is 100%. Barring sudden death, each one of us will go through the process of dying as an experience of life and notwithstanding the writing on the wall we shall seek its denial with whatever means at our disposal; dismissal of symptoms, preoccupation with trivialities, trust in our doctor, faith in God, metamorphosis, or belief in life after death. Naked and horizontal we shall expect more than platitudes from our physicians or surgeons— I wonder whether we will be satisfied. . . .

There is hardly a province of life from which concepts of domination are absent; mythology is preoccupied with it, history is a study of it, politics implements it. The genesis of man may well be related to the advent of the weapon, enabling him to control a hostile environment, for premeditated assault and domination. Spheres of conflict cover the globe; in every household there is dominant and dominated. What better setting, for domination, granted the best will in the world, than the naked frightened patient and the well-groomed, white-coated staff conferring with varying audibility at the end of the bed. We know so much more than the patient concerning the details of his or her illness that it is almost laughable. The patient cannot stand outside his diseased body and request a frank simplified account of his illness and its implications as if he were dealing with a broken-down car, because he is totally involved. How much do we concede in practice to this truism? How much do we endeavour to transcribe our findings into accessible terms? How often do you ask a patient whether he has any questions which he would like to ask? How much do we allow our advantageous position to gown us in the robes of autocrats, albeit benevolent and judging our management in the patient's best interest, but absolute rulers nonetheless over our patients—our subjects?

From "Motivation in Medicine" by Michael S. Rose
(*The Lancet*, 10 September (1966))

1 The story is told of a phone call made to a hospital about a patient. "How is Mr. Thorogood, Mr. Clifford Thorogood?" "When will he have his operation?" "When do you think he'll be leaving hospital?" The questioner more or less satisfied with her answers, the Ward Sister asked, "Whom shall I say called?" "Oh, this *is* Mr. Clifford Thorogood speaking. I'm using the public telephone in the entrance hall. Had to find out somehow!"

Is there any evidence that some medical practitioners and hospital authorities are doing their best to manifest their concern for "man as an individual"—as a sentient, anxious being? What more could be done? Should all doctors and nurses have a sound education in psychology?

2 Most people in the professions—doctors, lawyers, teachers in especial—inevitably assume positions of domination over others. Do the "others" really want it this way, preferring dependence, in spite of their mutterings? What safeguards exist to prevent the abuse of power? Should there be more?

3 We are educated for work, for marriage, for child-raising, for leisure, for retirement. Why not for death? What forms could such an education take? Would it really help? What guidance could the Churches offer?

4 "How much do we concede in practice to this truism?"

Do you agree that nowadays we emphasize principle at the expense of action? That we love to identify a problem, analyse it, even propose solutions to it—then hurriedly turn to another problem instead of doing something about the first? That somehow recognition of an evil, condemnation of an abuse, is enough to appease our troubled consciences? Have the mass media anything to do with this tendency?

THE RUSSIAN physiologist, Pavlov, died in 1936 at the age of eighty-six. His early observations are well known. Teach a dog to expect its dinner every time a lamp lights up and in due course the connection between light and food becomes fixed in its mind and its mouth will water when the lamp goes on, whether there is any dinner or not. Training of this kind can be applied to the minds of men as well as dogs; a practised cyclist rides a bicycle successfully "without thinking"; a competent pianist can react "automatically" to the marks on the page of music in front of him; a baby can be taught to pass water at the touch of a cold pot on its buttocks. But Pavlov's more advanced work on the mechanistic working of the brain was done later in life and its influence of all others bites most savagely on the minds of half the world's population.

It is a simple scientific experiment to "condition" a dog to expect food when it feels a weak electric current run through its leg. The current itself is almost pleasurable—do not children play with "shock" machines in fun fairs?—and its association with feeding makes it more so. But then the experimenter, bit by bit and day be day, increases the voltage of the current. Sharp and revolting pain is the price to be paid for food. The mind of the dog, tortured with pain and fear and hope and bewilderment, eventually breaks down.

This experiment was performed on a number of occasions and in a number of ways. A dog could be trained to expect food when a certain signal was given, for example, when a light was turned on or a buzzer buzzed. The connection between the signal and the reward was patiently and laboriously built up in its mind. But then Pavlov began to make the dog wait. The buzzer would sound or the light go on but there was a delay before the expected meal appeared. And this delay was made longer and longer. There was the dog, hungry and tired, the learned signal received—and it had to wait, tense, frustrated, slavering with anticipation, disappointed in its deepest hopes. Until at last its mind gave way again. . . .

We modern people have come to believe that the methods of the Inquisition were horrible. For a start, they were unscientific. Nevertheless, the tortures and imprisonment and the ceaseless questioning were an application in a rough and ready empirical form of the techniques later scientifically developed for dogs by Pavlov. And the purpose of the Inquisitors, although we may consider it to have been misguided, was a noble one. It was to bring the minds of the people they were working on back to a belief in the true faith, without which they would not only be deprived of the felicities of Heaven but would find themselves subject to the far more painful and prolonged tortures of Hell. The object of the technique applied by the Inquisitors was to change people's minds. Their methods were unscientific and sometimes—but not always—unsuccessful because the environmental pressures of those days, whatever they may have implied about the nature of God, were based on the assumption that men's minds were reflections of individual living souls. Today, the scientific atmosphere brings us to think that, in men as in dogs, minds are mechanisms of a certain sort that can be impressed with ideas in a certain way and, if required, can be broken down in another certain way so that the set of ideas on them can be taken off and new ones put on. . . .

But though science can be used to change minds, though it has to be admitted that a mind is a machine that can be broken down, that in fact any mind, no matter how loyal or strong or brave, can be brought to the point of unsaying the convictions and beliefs to which it has always held and made to profess beliefs and ideas that it previously abhorred—whether it be the mind of a Cardinal Midszenty of Hungary or Colonel Schwable of the United States Marines—in spite of all this and in spite of the persuasive pressure to believe that the purpose of modern society is no absenteeism and increased industrial productivity, there are still people whose lives follow a different path. . . .

Here and there are artists and dreamers, a very few philosophers, and even some who cling to ideas of noble deeds and honourable action apart altogether from technological efficiency. Dotted about in our society are those whose standards of life are distinct altogether from the "standard of living". . . .

Dr. Meerloo, who was once Chief of the Psychological Department of the Netherlands armed forces and now teaches psychiatry at Columbia University, does not deny that scientific knowledge is now available by which any mind can be overwhelmed. Hunger, lack of sleep, ill-usage and constant skilled repetition, repetition, repetition, mixed appropriately with unkindness, kindness, and unkindness—exactly as applied to the laboratory dogs—will in the end make any mind admit that black is white if this is the purpose of the operation. But there is no special cause for despair about this. Industrial society is widely equipped with machinery that destroys the bodies of those who use it, whether the machinery takes the form of thermo-nuclear weapons or automobiles on the highway. Why then should we be alarmed at the equally effective techniques that are capable of disrupting minds? Men and women have been found prepared to confront the physical force of science. Dr. Meerloo points out that the great and courageous minds for the future who will defy the spirit of conformity implicit in materialism and the highly efficient practical processes that are also now available to make them conform will be those possessed of spiritual bravery.

From *The Science Myth* by Magnus Pyke

1 Give instances of some ways in which you have been conditioned and consider the conditioning processes used. Choose examples at the levels of habit, belief, and attitude.
   Have you ever deliberately tried to condition somebody else? For what ends?

2 What are the most powerful agents of conformism or social conditioning? Is there any difference between "the organization man", "the true naval man", and "the devoted civil servant"?
   Is it possible to draw the line between loyalty, co-operation, selfishness, and unquestioning obedience?

3 Have the social scientists and psychologists engaged in motivational

research for the advertising industry any moral responsibility for the uses to which their findings are put? Is "the teenage revolution" a monstrous commercial confidence trick?

4 What ethical questions are raised by the introduction of programmed learning in schools and colleges?

5 Adolf Hitler used conditioning techniques (propaganda, parades, fear, and rewards) to get the German people to support his evil ambitions. In order to combat such an efficient, dedicated fighting machine as Germany, the British people, too, were conditioned, albeit in somewhat different ways. Did the circumstances justify this conditioning? What circumstances might warrant it again? Who would decide?

6 Why did the Western powers make such a fuss of Boris Pasternak and *Dr. Zhivago*? Who are the Pasternaks of our own society? Whence spring the reserves of character, intellect, or spirit that enable such men to raise their heads above the crowd?

MR. FOTHERINGAY decided to consult Mr. Maydig immediately after the service. So soon as that was determined, he found himself wondering why he had not done so before. . . .

"You don't believe, I suppose, that some common sort of person— like myself, for instance—as it might be sitting here now, might have some sort of twist inside him that made him able to do things by his will."

"It's possible," said Mr. Maydig. "Something of the sort, perhaps, is possible."

"If I might make free with something here, I think I might show you by a sort of experiment," said Mr. Fotheringay. "Now, take that tobacco-jar on the table, for instance. What I want to know is whether what I am going to do with it is a miracle or not. Just half a minute, Mr. Maydig, please."

He knitted his brows, pointed to the tobacco-jar and said: "Be a bowl of vi'lets."

The tobacco-jar did as it was ordered.

Mr. Maydig started violently at the change, and stood looking from the thaumaturgist to the bowl of flowers. He said nothing. Presently he ventured to lean over the table and smell the violets; they were fresh-picked and very fine ones. Then he stared at Mr. Fotheringay again.

"How did you do that?" he asked.

Mr. Fotheringay pulled his moustache. "Just told it—and there you are. Is that a miracle, or is it black art, or what is it? And what do you think's the matter with me? That's what I want to ask."

"It's a most extraordinary occurrence."

"And this day last week I knew no more that I could do things like that than you did. It came quite sudden. It's something odd about my will, I suppose, and that's as far as I can see."

"Is that—the only thing. Could you do other things besides that?"

"Lord, yes!" said Mr. Fotheringay. "Just anything." He thought, and suddenly recalled a conjuring entertainment he had seen. "Here!" he pointed, "change into a bowl of fish—no, not that—change into a glass bowl full of water with goldfish swimming in it. That's better! You see that, Mr. Maydig?"

"It's astonishing. It's incredible. You are either a most extra-ordinary . . . But no—"

"I could change it into anything," said Mr. Fotheringay. "Just anything. Here! be a pigeon, will you?"

In another moment a blue pigeon was fluttering round the room and making Mr. Maydig duck every time it came near him. "Stop there, will you?" said Mr. Fotheringay; and the pigeon hung motion-less in the air. "I could change it back to a bowl of flowers," he said, and after he had replaced the pigeon on the table worked that miracle. "I expect you will want your pipe in a bit," he said, and restored the tobacco-jar.

Mr. Maydig had followed all these later changes in a sort of ejaculatory silence. He stared at Mr. Fotheringay and in a very gingerly manner picked up the tobacco-jar, examined it, replaced it on the table. "Well!" was the only expression of his feelings. . . .

"A gift of working miracles—apparently a very powerful gift," said Mr. Maydig. "My dear sir, you are a most important man—a man of the most astonishing possibilities. As evidence, for example! And in other ways, the things you may do. . . ."

"Yes, I've thought of a thing or two," said Mr. Fotheringay. "But—some of the things came a bit twisty. You saw that fish at first? Wrong sort of bowl and wrong sort of fish. And I thought I'd ask someone."

"A proper course," said Mr. Maydig, "a very proper course." He stopped and looked at Mr. Fotheringay. "It's practically an unlimited gift. Let us test your powers, for instance. If they really are . . . If they really are all they seem to be."

And so, incredible as it may seem, in the study of the little house behind the Congregational Chapel, on the evening of Sunday, Nov. 10, 1896, Mr. Fotheringay, egged on and inspired by Mr. Maydig, began to work miracles. . . .

The small hours found Mr. Maydig and Mr. Fotheringay careering across the chilly market square under the still moon, in a sort of ecstasy of thaumaturgy, Mr. Maydig all flap and gesture, Mr. Fotheringay short and bristling, and no longer abashed at his greatness. They had reformed every drunkard in the Parliamentary division, changed all the beer and alcohol to water (Mr. Maydig had overruled Mr. Fotheringay on this point); they had, further, greatly improved the railway communication of the place, drained Flinder's swamp, improved the soil of One Tree Hill, and cured the vicar's wart. And they were going to see what could be done with the injured pier at South Bridge. "The place," gasped Mr. Maydig, "won't be the same place tomorrow. How surprised and thankful everyone will be!" And just at that moment the church clock struck three.

"I say," said Mr. Fotheringay, "that's three o'clock! I must be getting back. I've got to be at business by eight. And besides Mrs. Wimms...."

Mr. Maydig gripped his arm suddenly. His eyes were bright and wild. "My dear chap," he said, "there's no hurry. Look"—he pointed to the moon at the zenith—"Joshua!"

"Joshua?" said Mr. Fotheringay.

"Joshua," said Mr. Maydig. "Why not? Stop it."

Mr. Fotheringay looked at the moon.

"That's a bit tall," he said, after a pause.

"Why not?" said Mr. Maydig. "Of course it doesn't stop. You stop the rotation of the earth, you know. Time stops. It isn't as if we were doing harm."

"H'm!" said Mr. Fotheringay. "Well," he sighed, "I'll try. Here!"

He buttoned up his jacket and addressed himself to the habitable globe, with as good an assumption of confidence as lay in his power. "Jest stop rotating, will you?" said Mr. Fotheringay.

Incontinently he was flying head over heels through the air at the rate of dozens of miles a minute. . . .

> From "The Man Who Could Work Miracles"
> by H. G. Wells

1 Many men today wield powers, that, though not of a supernatural order, might seem miraculous to colossi of previous age. Caesar would boggle at the powers of the President of the United States; Genghis Khan would wonder at the worship of Mao Tse Tung; Tamburlaine would disbelieve the destructive power in the hands of a Polaris submarine.

Who are the really powerful people today? Should individual men be entrusted with such powers? How can men prepare themselves for such burdens? How should they be selected—and how removed?

2 Technology translates knowledge into power at an accelerating speed. Yearly we are provided with more new things, more new situations, that we do not know how to cope with or to integrate with the pattern of living; the motor car, television, contraceptive pills, computers present us with incalculable problems as well as incalculable benefits. As technology is powered by the irresistible impetus of demand, should we then attempt to control material progress by programming very carefully the search for new knowledge?

3 Freedom of inquiry has long been regarded as one of the essential freedoms. But is it? Does it ever conflict with the other vital liberties? Do we need now to consider more carefully those conditions under which the law holds true, and identify those conditions where it does not?

4 Many people nowadays—especially popular entertainers—are given the illusion of power because of the tremendous efficiency of the machinery of celebrity manufacture. Does this artificial situation harm the idols? Does it harm the fans? How can we grow out of it?

5 *Must* absolute power corrupt absolutely?

In the hour before dawn one day in the summer of 1945, the hills of the Jornada del Muerto, a desert stretch in New Mexico, were briefly lighted with a light no man had ever seen before. We who were there knew that a new world lay before us. . . .

Let me be clear on one point: no great new principle of nature was discovered or revealed in that first atomic explosion. The bomb which we there tested was based on the broad foundation of a century of physical science. In its design were embodied the great principles of the behaviour of radiation and matter, as they were worked out in the closing years of the last century and in the first three decades of this. . . .

If there was any surprise in this first explosion, it lay not in any great new discovery. It lay rather in the fact that what happened was like what we thought would happen—that the physical science which had been built into this new weapon was such a sure and reliable guide. . . .

For the field of physics there will be new possibilities. I may give one example: the neutron is a constituent of atomic nuclei, but it does not occur free in nature, where its properties can be studied. Neutrons do occur in great numbers among the fragments of chain-reacting systems, and it is there that their somewhat unfamiliar behaviour will be best explored. Of this whole field of research we see very much less than the mariner sees of the iceberg. That is what is meant by research.

The explosion in New Mexico was neither a controlled source of power nor a research tool—it was a weapon. Within a few weeks it was to be a weapon used against human targets in the strikes of August 6th and 9th, 1945. Today this is the aspect of the atomic age which is most prominent—and most rightly prominent—in all our thoughts.

There does not seem to be any valid doubt that atomic weapons can be made, made plentifully, made cheaply, and indeed be made very much more destructive than the one we tested in New Mexico. There does not seem to be any valid hope that defences against such weapons can be made effective against attack based on surprise, or that specific defences against such weapons, other than the destruction of enemy bases and enemy carriers, will be developed in the future. There is, to my mind, little valid foundation for the belief that in a world torn by major wars these weapons, for tactical or humane reasons, will be left unexploited.

Often before, men have claimed that a weapon had been found so terrible that wars would cease. Often before, men have pointed to the increasing technical and social interdependence of the peoples of the world and argued that wars should cease. The fact that these arguments have not prevailed does not mean that they will not prevail today.

The fact that increasingly terrible wars have been waged does not mean that we should prepare to wage still more terrible ones in he future. It is not in this sense that history is to be read. For this is what is new in the atomic age : a world to be united, in law, in common understanding, in common humanity, before a common peril.

From "It was a Weapon" by J. Robert Oppenheimer

1 How would you describe Oppenheimer's attitude to the first atomic bomb: is he proud of it, humbled by it, ashamed of it, excited by it, reassured by it, or afraid of it?

2 Does this scientist advance any reasons for the prediction voiced in the last two paragraphs?

3 What was the moral dilemma confronting the scientists and technologists who worked to produce the atomic bomb during the 1939–1945 war? Was this dilemma of a different order from the moral problem confronting scientists and technologists engaged in current space research programmes?

4 Concentration camp officials who put people into gas chambers are still being rounded up and punished for what they did. What of the men who built the gas chambers—or the men who designed them? How far does the responsibility for evil spread?

5 Are scientists the only seekers after truth who risk promoting great harm as well as great good? What about artists and law-makers? Have scientists a special responsibility for separating their own humanity from their professional role?

MR. TANIMOTO and Mr. Matsuo took their way through the shopping centre, already full of people, and across two of the rivers to the sloping streets of Koi, and up them to the outskirts and foothills. As they started up a valley away from the tight-ranked houses, the all-clear sounded. (The Japanese radar operators, detecting only three planes, supposed that they comprised a reconnaissance.) Pushing the handcart up to the rayon man's house was tiring, and the men, after they had manoeuvred their load into the driveway and to the front steps, paused to rest a while. They stood with a wing of the house between them and the city. Like most homes in this part of Japan, the house consisted of a wooden frame and wooden walls supporting a heavy tile roof. Its front hall, packed with rolls of bedding and clothing, looked like a cool cave full of fat cushions. Opposite the house, to the right of the front door, there was a large, finicky rock garden. There was no sound of planes. The morning was still; the place was cool and pleasant.

Then a tremendous flash of light cut across the sky. Mr. Tanimoto has a distinct recollection that it travelled from east to west, from the city towards the hills. It seemed a sheet of sun. Both he and Mr. Matsuo reacted in terror—and both had time to react (for they were 3,500 yards, or two miles, from the centre of the explosion). Mr. Matsuo dashed up the front steps into the house and dived among the bedrolls and buried himself there. Mr. Tanimoto took four or five steps and threw himself between two big rocks in the garden. He bellied up very hard against one of them. As his face was against the stone, he did not see what happened. He felt a sudden pressure, and splinters and pieces of board and fragments of tile fell on him. He heard no roar. (Almost no one in Hiroshima recalls hearing any noise of the bomb. But a fisherman in his sampan on the Inland Sea near Tsuzu, the man with whom Mr. Tanimoto's mother-in-law and sister-in-law were living, saw the flash and heard a tremendous explosion; he was nearly twenty miles from Hiroshima, but the thunder was greater than when the B-29s hit Iwakuni, only five miles away.)

When he dared, Mr. Tanimoto raised his head and saw that the rayon man's house had collapsed. He thought a bomb had fallen directly on it. Such clouds of dust had risen that there was a sort of twilight around. In panic, not thinking for the moment of Mr. Matsuo under the ruins, he dashed out into the street. He noticed as he ran that the concrete wall of the estate had fallen over—towards the house rather than away from it. In the street, the first thing he saw was a squad of soldiers who had been burrowing into the hillside opposite, making one of the thousands of dugouts in which the Japanese apparently intended to resist invasion, hill by hill, life for life; the soldiers were coming out of the hole, where they should have been safe, and blood was running from their heads, chests, and backs. They were silent and dazed.

Under what seemed to be a local dust cloud, the day grew darker and darker. . . .

Mr. Tanimoto, fearful for his family and church, at first ran towards them by the shortest route, along Koi Highway. He was the only person making his way into the city; he met hundreds and hundreds who were fleeing, and every one of them seemed to be hurt in some way. The eyebrows of some were burned off and skin hung from their faces and hands. Others, because of pain, held their arms up as if carrying something in both hands. Some were vomiting as they walked. Many were naked or in shreds of clothing. On some undressed bodies, the burns had made patterns—of undershirt straps and suspenders and, on the skin of some women (since white repelled the heat from the bomb and dark clothes absorbed it and conducted it to the skin), the shapes of flowers they had had on their kimonos. Many, although injured themselves, supported relatives who were worse off. Almost all had their heads bowed, looked straight ahead, were silent, and showed no expression whatever.

After crossing Koi Bridge and Kannon Bridge, having run the whole way, Mr. Tanimoto saw, as he approached the centre, that all the houses had been crushed and many were afire. Here the trees were bare and their trunks charred. He tried at several points to penetrate the ruins, but the flames always stopped him. Under many houses, people screamed for help, but no one helped; in general, survivors that day assisted only their relatives or immediate neighbours, for they could not comprehend or tolerate a wider circle of misery. The wounded limped past the screams, and Mr. Tanimoto ran past them. As a Christian he was filled with compassion for those who were trapped, and as a Japanese he was overwhelmed by the shame of being unhurt, and he prayed as he ran, "God help them and take them out of the fire."

From Hiroshima by John Hersey

1   "If humanity destroys itself, it will be because of failure of the imagination." When the news of the dropping of the bomb on Hiroshima
came through, many people in this country rejoiced. Of what were
they guilty?
Many people in this country are indifferent to the nation's possession
of nuclear arms. Of what are they guilty?
Many people who denounce nuclear warfare will countenance other
means of warfare—provided that the cause is just. Of what are they
guilty?
How can we live, but by the truth?

Part Seven

Education

WHEN I taught biology I spent many hours designing experiments for the practical classes which would "work". And I was successful. They did work. Students came into the laboratory from 2 p.m. to 5 p.m. and succeeded in getting results from experiments which had taken me weeks to achieve. What they didn't succeed in getting was the essential experience of all experimental work : that it doesn't come off the first time; that unless the temperature is just right, and the plant in just the right condition (and we always made sure from the instruction sheet that all these conditions were just right) the experiment doesn't come off at all. Again (and I admit it's inevitable) formal laboratory education is designed to protect the student from many of the frustrations and exasperations of science. This gives rise to an illusion that when you've done a course in (say) biology, you've mastered the techniques of biology. Of course you've made a start; but remember that this ancient process of education is not a full picture of real life; it's an anthology from real life. If you were, for instance, a member of the Mende tribe in Sierra Leone, your education would consist of a long series of initiations—extending over years—into what Americans call "real-life situations". You would learn to endure pain by suffering pain. You would learn to feed yourself in the bush by being put out into the bush without food. In our institutionalized education the danger—and of course it's inevitable: I'm not advocating a retreat to tribal education—is that apprenticeship for life is ousted by a course of instruction set by a syllabus. Ordeal by initiation shrivels into ordeal by examination. . . .

Unless you continue to be a student your horizons of knowledge will remain exactly as they are today, fixed by today's curriculum and examination syllabus. [A man's training is the foundation of his skill in his profession, and he cannot be expected to welcome any discovery which undermines that foundation.] Yet obsolescence is built into that training, as surely as it is into the lines of a flashy new car. . . .

Do you know the story of the Sabre Tooth Curriculum? It concerns a palaeolithic tribe who, realizing that their survival depended on keeping at bay sabre-tooth tigers and catching fish by hand in the clear pools, invented education. Their children, instead of whiling away their time at play, were taught the art of scaring tigers by fire and of fish-grabbing by hand from the pools. The invention was a great success. The children loved it and the tribe flourished.

Then the climate changed. A great glacier came down the valley where the tribe lived. The sabre-tooth tigers vanished. In their place came bears who were not afraid of fire and could not be scared that way. And the pools became so muddy that fish could no longer be seen and caught with bare hands. It was not long before tribesmen of initiative and resource had adapted themselves to these new circumstances. They discovered they could trap bears by digging pits in the forest tracks and they discovered that they could catch fish in the muddy pools by using nets. Once more they are masters of their contemporary environment.

But schools still continued to teach the arts of tiger-scaring and fish-grabbing. The education authority even succeeded in capturing an old tiger further down the valley and keeping him in a cage so that the children should have practical material to work on. Then some radical suggested that these useless skills should be dropped from the curriculum and that in their place schools should learn fish-net making and the digging of bear pits.

The suggestion was received in horror by the authorities. To teach fish-net making and the digging of bear pits: that would not be education; that would be mere vocational training. It will be a bad day for our schools (they said) when we drop the fundamental cultural subjects of tiger-scaring and fish-grabbing. Of course no one would dream of grabbing fish in real life these days, and there are no tigers to scare; but these subjects are rich in the traditions of our tribe; they teach principles of courage and taste. The curriculum is already over-full and we cannot (they said) introduce subjects like fish-net making and bear catching, which are of no cultural value.

From a lecture by Sir Eric Ashby, F.R.S.,
to the School of Pharmacy, London University, in 1961

1   In what sense is education "an anthology from real life"? How can the reality of life situations be preserved in, say, a course in biology, or in government, or in drama? Are all studies *concerned with* preparation for "real life"? What real-life experiences does education usually neglect, though it would be helpful to have some preparation for them? Can education offer effective substitutes for "ordeal by initiation"?

2   What purpose does an examination serve? Why have we come to rely so much upon examinations and to value so highly the certificates they yield? Is the examination, with its concomitant syllabus, inevitably an agent of curriculum conservation? Could we make more use of other forms of assessment?

3   How can education foster a man's ability to recognize in later life that his techniques are obsolete and his knowledge inadequate—and his willingness to do something about it? Is it enough to lay on refresher courses or to provide facilities for industrial retraining?

4   What is really involved in the parable of the Sabre Tooth Curriculum? Is the implied parallel a fair one? Does it make a satisfactory distinction between education and training?

5 Can you suggest criteria that could be referred to when decisions have to be made about curriculum conservation or development? Who, at present, makes these decisions? Should more attention be paid to student opinion in such matters?

6 Do developments in teaching methods affect the content of the curriculum? What methods suit you best? What other methods would you like to experience?

THE FATHER of Blaise Pascal was a member of a well-to-do family, and was one of the most important government officials in Central France. He was well known as a mathematician, and an expert in mechanics. He was described by Bishop as a "competent executive, an imperious father, sacrificing himself for his children, and requiring their sacrifices as his right, utterly honest, but demanding all his due, jealously proud of his achievement, of his family, of his small nobility". He had four children, of whom three survived—two girls and a boy, Blaise. He found in the rapid and extraordinary development of his children's intelligence an interest more absorbing than all his worldly success. When Blaise was seven his father relinquished his post in order to devote all his time to his children's education. The boy's mother had died when he was three.

Etienne, the father of Blaise, had unorthodox views on education, considering that the exercise of reason was more important than the routine of Latin grammar. He wanted the boy to learn reason and judgement, and to learn the nature of a fact and its value. "Information was to come to him," wrote Bishop, "as an answer to curiosity, as a reward for the desire to know." He taught history, geography and philosophy during meals, and devised games to illustrate the principles. His principal maxim was to keep the boy superior to his tasks—that he should never let the work get him down, by being rushed or overloaded with knowledge. It was for this reason that he wanted his children to learn classics before mathematics. The whole course of education was carefully planned in advance.

"He showed him what languages are, their organization and purpose, how they have been reduced to grammar in the form of rules, how these rules came to have exceptions, and how the correspondences of the languages have permitted men to transfer their thoughts from one linguistic conglomerate to another. He showed him the reason for grammatical rules, so that when he came to learn grammar, he knew why he was doing so, and applied himself precisely to those things which needed the most application."

The curriculum included civic and canon law as well as religious and ecclesiastical history. In science the boy learned insensibly the principles of the experimental method, observing, classifying, and proposing generalizations from his evidence. "From his childhood," says Gilberte, "he could not surrender except to what seemed to him evidently true, so that when he was not given good reasons, he sought them out himself, and when he had become interested in something, he would not quit it until he had found a reason which could satisfy him." Mortimer wrote that "always and in everything the truth was the one goal in his mind, and nothing short of it contented him. . . ." On one occasion someone at table accidentally struck a porcelain plate with a knife and it made a sound. Blaise noticed this and saw that when the plate was touched the sound stopped. At once he wanted to know why, and this led him to make other experiments in sound."

Bishop added that Blaise's precocity upset his father's educational scheme. When Blaise heard friends talk about geometry, he asked what geometry was. His father replied that it was the noblest and highest form of a man's knowledge. Blaise felt ill-used because he had not been taught this, and begged and pleaded for instruction, "whining for mathematics as another would whine for candy". His father refused, for he thought that the mathematics would distract him from classics, and forbade his son to think or speak of it again. He promised him mathematics as soon as he knew Latin and Greek. He locked up his textbooks and cautioned his friends not to mention mathematics in the boy's presence. All that Blaise could gather was that geometry was the science of making true diagrams, and of finding the proportions between them. Thinking about this, he began to make charcoal diagrams on the floor. He noted certain evident truths and axioms. He set himself problems and devised satisfactory methods of proof or demonstrations. He proceeded from step to step until he reached the thirty-second proposition of Euclid that the angles in a triangle together equal two right angles. His father chanced to enter the room and stood and watched for a time without Blaise knowing he was there. On questioning, Blaise explained the structure of his logic with his own terminology. His father Etienne did not say a word: he left the room and wept tears of joy to a friend. He unlocked the Euclid and gave it to the boy. The boy learned Latin and geometry together, mastering the science in his playtime. Four years later (at sixteen) he produced his essay on conic sections, in which he progressed beyond the mathematical knowledge of his century, and heralded modern projective geometry.

Etienne was a member of the Académie Libre which met weekly to discuss scientific matters. He introduced Blaise to this body, and

Blaise absorbed ideas and teachings there. At nineteen he invented and constructed the first calculating machine. He gave Pascal's law to physics, proved the existence of the vacuum, and helped to establish the science of hydrodynamics. He created the mathematical theory of probability. His prose style influenced French literary language. Subsequently he wrote his *Pensées*, thoughts which "affected the mental cast of three centuries". He died at thirty-nine, after a life of invalidism. . . .

From Blaise Pascal by E. Mortimer

1 Should parents be free to determine the course of their children's education, or should the State decide? What problems stem from the principle "equality of opportunity in education"?

2 In your own education, has information been presented as an answer for curiosity or as a means of stifling it? In what ways has your curiosity been deliberately stimulated? Do you think that the teacher's job has become easier or more difficult as you have got older?

3 "His principal maxim was to keep the boy superior to his tasks." Is this a practicable maxim with a *class* of students? What do you consider to be the optimum size of a class? Do you think that the evils of over-large classes have been over-stressed?

4 Pascal was a genius. Is it equally useful for a boy of moderate ability to be given reasons for all his learning, to be shown how the new bit fits into the overall picture?

5 Even the curriculum devised by Etienne Pascal proved inadequate. Why are curricula devised and imposed? What principles should underlie their formulation? Should there always be scope for student choice—and rejection?

6 By what can we judge the success of Pascal's education?

AN ASSEMBLAGE of learned men, zealous for their own sciences, and rivals of each other, are brought, by familiar intercourse and for the sake of intellectual peace, to adjust together the claims and relations of their respective subjects of investigation. They learn to respect, to consult, to aid each other. Thus is created a pure and clear atmosphere of thought, which the student also breathes, though in his own case he only pursues a few sciences out of the multitude. He profits by an intellectual tradition, which is independent of particular teachers, which guides him in his choice of subjects, and duly interprets for him those which he chooses. He apprehends the great outlines of knowledge, the principles on which it rests, the scale of its parts, its lights and its shades, its great points and its little, as he otherwise cannot apprehend them. Hence it is that his education is called "Liberal". A habit of mind is formed which lasts through life, of which the attributes are, freedom, equitableness, calmness, moderation, and wisdom; or what in a former Discourse I have ventured to call a philosophical habit. This then I would assign as the special fruit of the education furnished at a University, as contrasted with other places of teaching or modes of teaching. This is the main purpose of a University in its treatment of its students.

And now the question is asked me, What is the use of it? And my answer will constitute the main subject of the Discourses which are to follow.

Cautious and practical thinkers, I say, will ask of me, what, after all, is the gain of this Philosophy, of which I make such account, and from which I promise so much. Even supposing it to enable us to give the degree of confidence exactly due to every science respectively, and to estimate precisely the value of every truth which is anywhere to be found, how are we better for this master view of things, which I have been extolling? Does it not reverse the principle of the division of labour? will practical objects be obtained better or worse by its cultivation? to what then does it lead? where does it end? what does it do? how does it profit? what does it promise? Particular sciences are respectively the basis of definite arts, which carry onto results tangible and beneficial the truths which are the subjects of the knowledge attained; what is the Art of this science of sciences? what is the fruit of such a Philosophy? what are we proposing to effect, what inducements do we hold out to the Catholic community, when we set about the enterprise of founding a University?

I am asked what is the end of University Education, and of the Liberal or Philosophical Knowledge which I conceive it to impart: I answer, that what I have already said has been sufficient to show that it has a very tangible, real, and sufficient end, though the end cannot be divided from that knowledge itself. Knowledge is capable of being its own end. Such is the constitution of the human mind, that any kind of knowledge, if it be really such, is its own reward. And if this is true of all knowledge, it is true also of that special Philosophy, which I have made to consist in a comprehensive view of truth in all its branches, of the relations of science to science, of their mutual bearings, and their respective values. What the worth of such an acquirement is, compared with other objects which we seek—wealth or power or honour or the conveniences and comforts of life, I do not profess here to discuss; but I would maintain, and mean to show, that it is an object, in its own nature so really and undeniably good, as to be the compensation of a great deal of thought in the compassing, and a great deal of trouble in the attaining. . . .

I consider Knowledge to have its end in itself. For all its friends, or its enemies, may say, I insist upon it, that it is as real a mistake to burden it with virtue or religion as with the mechanical arts. Its direct business is not to steel the soul against temptation, or to console it in affliction, any more than to set the loom in motion, or to direct the steam carriage; be it ever so much the means or the condition of both material and moral advancement, still, taken by and in itself, it as little mends our hearts as it improves our temporal circumstances. And if its eulogists claim for it such a power, they commit the very same kind of encroachment on a province not their own as the political economist who should maintain that his science educated him for casuistry or diplomacy. Knowledge is one thing, virtue is another; good sense is not conscience, refinement is not humility, nor is largeness and justness of view faith. Philosophy, however enlightened, however profound, gives no command over the passions, no influential motives, no vivifying principles. Liberal Education makes not the Christian, not the Catholic, but the gentleman. It is well to be a gentleman, it is well to have a cultivated intellect, a delicate taste, a candid, equitable, dispassionate mind, noble and courteous bearing in the conduct of life;—these are the connatural qualities of a large knowledge; they are the objects of a University; I am advocating, I shall illustrate and insist upon them; but still I repeat, they are no guarantee for sanctity or even for conscientiousness, they may attach to the man of the world, to the profligate, to the heartless—pleasant, alas, and attractive as he shows when decked out in them. Taken by themselves, they do but seem to be what they are not; they look like virtue at a distance, but they are detected by close observers, and on the long run; and hence it is that they are popularly accused of pretence and hypocrisy, not, I repeat, from their own fault, but because their professors and their admirers persist in taking them for what they are not, and are officious in arrogating for them a praise to which they have no claim. Quarry the granite rock with razors, or moor the vessel with a thread of silk; then may you hope with such keen and delicate instruments as human knowledge and human reason to contend against these giants, the passion and the pride of man.

From *The Idea of a University*
by John Henry Newman

1 What does Newman mean when he uses the words: science; art; gentleman?

2 Newman's ideal of "an assemblege of learned men", engaged in familiar intercourse, respecting, consulting, and aiding each other, was based on the leisurely communion of scholars living in numerically small Oxford colleges in the mid-nineteenth century. What problems confront a modern university trying to live up to this ideal? How might it attempt to overcome them? Or have our universities adopted other ideals?

3 In what respects do currently accepted criteria of a liberal education differ from or add to the main criterion advanced by Newman? What are the reasons for the development of the definition?

4 "Would you rather own a television set; have the skill to repair it; or understand the nature of radio waves?" Does this comparison of incomparables bring us any nearer to an understanding of the doctrine, "knowledge for its own sake"?

5 Is it still possible for the man specializing in one or two subjects to apprehend as well "the great outlines of knowledge, the principles on which it rests, the scale of its parts, its lights and its shades, its great points and its little"? Take one of your own specialisms: could you identify its principal concepts and methods of working, analysis, or inquiry? Would it be possible to introduce these to another student, whose mind is enlivened by study in another specialism, without requiring of him the heavy study commitments that his first specialism has entailed?

6 Is a balanced curriculum up to first degree level of more educational worth than specialization at the age of 15 plus minority-time liberal or complementary studies? Should liberal studies concentrate on the interdisciplinary, topic approach? Could this constitute a practical first approach to "that special Philosophy" that Newman so values and thus describes: "a comprehensive view of truth in all its branches, of the relations of science to science, of their mutual bearing, and their respective values"?

MY INNER story is exceedingly simple, if not indeed dull: my life has been devoted to science and my only real ambition has been to contribute to it and live up to its standards. In complete contradiction to this, the external course has been rather bumpy. I finished school in feudal Hungary as the son of a wealthy landowner and I had no worries about my future. A few years later I find myself working in Hamburg, Germany, with a slight hunger oedema. In 1942 I find myself in Istanbul, involved in secret diplomatic activity with a setting fit for a cheap and exciting spy story. Shortly after, I get a warning that Hitler had ordered the Governor of Hungary to appear before him, screaming my name at the top of his voice and demanding my delivery. Arrest warrants were passed out even against members of my family. In my pocket I find a Swedish passport, having been made a full Swedish citizen on the order of the King of Sweden— I am "Mr. Swenson", my wife "Mrs. Swenson". Sometime later I find myself in Moscow, treated in the most royal fashion by the Government (with caviar three times a day), but it does not take long before I am declared "a traitor of the people" and I play the role of the villain on the stages of Budapest. At the same time, I am refused entrance to the USA for my Soviet sympathies. Eventually, I find peace at Woods Hole, Massachusetts, working in a solitary corner of the Marine Biology Laboratory. After some nerve-racking complications, due to McCarthy, things straightened out, but the internal struggle is not completely over. I am troubled by grave doubts about the usefulness of scientific endeavour and have a whole drawer filled with treatises on politics and their relation to science, written for myself with the sole purpose of clarifying my mind, and finding an answer to the question: will science lead to the elevation or destruction of man, and has my scientific endeavour any sense? . . .

On my Mother's side, I am the fourth generation of scientists. My Father was interested only in farming and so my Mother's influence prevailed. Music filled the house and the conversation at the table roamed about the intellectual achievements of the entire world. Politics and finance had no place in our thoughts. I am a scientist, myself, because at an early age I learned that only intellectual values were worth striving for, artistic or scientific creation being the highest aim. I strongly believe that we establish the co-ordinates of our evaluation at a very early age. What we do later depends on this scale of values which mostly cannot be changed later. We are somewhat like Dr. Lorenz' goose which has hatched at the foot of a chair and recognized the chair as its mother all its later life. This is important for education, in case we are not intending to produce only "corporation men" with their intellectual crew cuts.

I must have been a very dull child. Nothing happened to me. I read no books and needed private tutoring to pass my exams. Around puberty, something changed and I became a voracious reader and decided to become a scientist. My uncle, a noted histologist (M. Lenhossek), who dominated our family and was a precocious child himself, violently protested, seeing no future for such a dull youngster in science. When his opinion gradually improved, he consented to my going into cosmetics. Later, he even considered my becoming a dentist. When I finished high school with top marks, he admitted the possibility of my becoming a proctologist (specialist of anus and rectum; he had haemorrhoids). So my first scientific paper, written in the first year of my medical studies, dealt with the epithelium of the anus. I started science on the wrong end, but soon I shifted to the vitreous body, the fibrillar fine structure I explored with new methods.

I wanted to understand life but found the complexity of physiology overwhelming. So I shifted to pharmacology where, at least, one of the partners, the drug, was simple. This, I found, did not relieve the difficulty. So, I went into bacteriology, but found bacteria too complex, too. I shifted on, to physicochemistry and then to chemistry, that is, to molecules, the smallest units in those days. Ten years ago I found molecules too complex and shifted to electrons, hoping to have reached bottom. But Nature has no bottom: its most basic principle is "organization". If Nature puts two things together she produces something new with new qualities, which cannot be expressed in terms of qualities of the components. When going from electrons and protons to atoms, from here to molecules, molecular aggregates, etc., up to the cell or the whole animal, at every level we find something new, a new breathtaking vista. Whenever we separate two things, we lose something, something which may have been the most essential feature. So now, at 68, I am to work my way up again following electrons in their motion through more extensive systems, hoping to arrive, some day, at an understanding of the cellular level of organization. So the internal course of my life made a smooth sinusoid curve; not so the external course. . . .

After two years at Leiden, where I devoted my free time to learning chemistry, I joined Hamburger's Laboratory at Groningen where I worked for another four years. Salaries were very low but allowed for a very modest life, which was happy and quiet. . . . Hamburger's death made an end to all this. His successor was a psychologist who disliked chemistry and disliked me with it. I thought that I had to give up altogether, being still a beginner in science, who had no more money and no foreign diploma. So I sent my wife with my child back to Hungary to her parents and prepared for the end. I saw no chance left. For a farewell to science I went to attend the International Physiological Congress at Stockholm (1926). The presidential address was delivered by Sir Frederick Gowland Hopkins, who, to my surprise, mentioned my name three times, more than anyone else's. So, after his lecture I picked up all my courage and addressed him. "Why don't you come to Cambridge?" he asked. "I will see to it that you get a Rockefeller fellowship." And so he did. He was, and still is, a mystery to me. He was the man who had the most influence on my scientific development though I never talked to him about science and heard him speak but once or twice. His papers were not especially fascinating, yet he had a magic influence on the people around him. That little unassuming man, with all his childish vanity, was a humble searcher of truth. What his individuality proclaimed was that in spite of all the hard work involved, research is not a systematic occupation but an intuitive artistic vocation.

From "Lost in the Twentieth Century"
by Albert Szent-Gyorgyi

1   "I strongly believe that we establish the co-ordinates of our evaluation at a very early age." What is likely to influence us most in the establishment of those co-ordinates? Do you agree that this scale of values is unlikely to be modified later? Do we take infant education seriously enough?

2   What is the role of the Director of a Scientific Research Project? Did Diaghilev and Oppenheimer have anything at all in common? Is the author right to value artistic and scientific creation as the (equal first) highest aim? Why should he then have "grave doubts about the usefulness of scientific endeavour"?

3   Has the fuss about the "two cultures" given credence to a basically false dichotomy between science and the arts, or has it led to a number of essential educational reforms?

4   The author says that "the internal course of my life made a smooth sinusoid curve". Was this because he realized that his own scientific activities and his own continuing scientific education were inseparable? Can any man, whatever his vocation, afford to stop learning? Are those who have stopped learning dangerous to the rest of mankind?

ACKNOWLEDGMENTS

The author and publishers express their gratitude to the following for permission to reprint passages from copyright material:

The University of Chicago Press for "I think, therefore" by Richard H. Strauss from *Perspectives in Biology and Medicine*.

Charles T. Branford Co. Publishers, Newton, Mass., U.S.A. for the extract from *Bodily Changes in Pain, Hunger, Fear, and Rage* by Walter B. Cannon.

Dr. T. A. Lloyd Davies and the *Medical Journal of Malaya* for the extract from "Medicine, Society, and Health".

W. H. Freeman and Company for the extract from "The Hallucinogenic Drugs" by F. Barron, M. E. Jarvik, and S. Bunnell, Jr. in *Scientific American*.

Penguin Books Ltd for the extract from Rosemary Edmunds' translation of *Anna Karenina* by Leo Tolstoy.

W. H. Allen and Company for the extract from *Saturday Night and Sunday Morning* by Alan Sillitoe.

Laurence Pollinger Ltd for the extract from *Cider with Rosie* by Laurie Lee, published by The Hogarth Press Ltd.

Longmans, Green and Co. Limited for the extract from *English Social History* by G. M. Trevelyan.

John Wiley and Sons, Inc. for the extract from "Are the Social Sciences Really Historical?" by A. Donegan in *Delaware Seminar*, Vol. I.

Clarendon Press, Oxford, for the extract from *English History 1914-1945* by A. J. P. Taylor.

Mrs Laura Huxley and Chatto and Windus Ltd for the extract from *Brave New World* by Aldous Huxley.

Miss Sonia Brownell and Secker and Warburg Ltd for the extract from *Animal Farm* by George Orwell.

Routledge and Kegan Paul Ltd for the extract from *Science and Industry in the Nineteenth Century* by J. D. Bernal.

Faber and Faber Ltd for the extract from *The Idea of a Christian Society* by T. S. Eliot.

University of California Press for the extract from their translation of *Principia Mathematica Philosophica Naturalis* by Isaac Newton.

Methuen and Co. Ltd for the extract from *Relativity, the Special and General Theory* by A. Einstein.

Carnegie Institution of Washington for the extract from the Report of the President on the Sixtieth Anniversary of the Carnegie Institution for 1961-1962 by Caryl P. Haskins.

The New England Journal of Medicine for the extract from "Wound Healing and Vitamin C" by J. H. Crandon, C. C. Lind, and D. B. Dill.

Souvenir Press Ltd for the extract from "Science for the Good of Your Soul" by R. L. M. Synge in *The Science of Science* edited by Maurice Goldsmith.

Cambridge Udiversity Press for the extract from *Science and the Modern World* by A. N. Whitehead.

David Garnett and Chatto and Windus Ltd for the extract from *Lady into Fox* by David Garnett.

Gerald Duckworth and Co. Ltd for the extract from *The British Penal System* by R. S. E. Hinde.

The Editor of *The Lancet* for the extract from "Motivation in Medicine" by Michael S. Rose.

John Murray (Publishers) Ltd for the extract from *The Science Myth* by Magnus Pyke.

Executors of H. G. Wells for the extract from "The Man Who Could Work Miracles" in *The Collected Stories of H. G. Wells*.

John Murray (Publishers) Ltd for the extract from "It was a Weapon" by J. Robert Oppenheimer in *Autobiography of Science* edited by Forest Ray Moulton and Justus J. Schifferes.

Hamish Hamilton Ltd for the extract from *Hiroshima* by John Hersey.

Sir Eric Ashby, F.R.S., for the extract from his lecture to the School of Pharmacy, London University.

Methuen and Co. Ltd for the extract from *Blaise Pascal* by E. Mortimer.

Annual Reviews, Inc., for the extract from "Lost in the Twentieth Century" by Albert Szent-Gyorgyi in *Annual Review of Biochemistry* and *The Excitement and Fascination of Science*.